Amelia Reborn?
Egypt

BY

JULIA SVADIHATRA

Amelia Reborn?
Egypt
Copyright © 2009 by Julia SvadiHatra

iUniverse books may be ordered through booksellers or by contacting:

iUniverse
1663 Liberty Drive
Bloomington, IN 47403
www.iuniverse.com
1-800-Authors (1-800-288-4677)

ISBN: 978-1-4401-4108-9 (pbk)
ISBN: 978-1-4401-4109-6 (ebk)

Printed in the United States of America

Editor: Roxane Christ - www.1steditor.biz

Cover design Most4u.net

Photo of Sphinx by Laurean Darlene SV

iUniverse rev. date: 11/2/2009

Dedication

Dedicated to the creativity of the people who lived on Earth or will be living in the future.

Leonardo Da Vinci, Wolfgang Amadeus Mozart, Alexander Pushkin, Johann Sebastian Bach, Tchaikovsky, Lev Tolstoy, *Michelangelo, Rembrandt van Rijn,* George Friedrich Händel, Alfons Ven, "Abba", Elvis Presley, Rimsky Korsakov, *Albert Einstein,* "Enigma", *Galileo Galilee, Nicolaus Copernicus,* Nostradamus, Tesla, Mendeleyev, Marie Curie, Louis Pasteur, Stephen Hawking, *Jan Van Hyusum, Jan Davidsz de Heem, Edward Grieg,* Peter Breughel Pierre-Auguste Renoir, Frans Snyders, William Shakespeare, conductor Igor Golovchin, actor Jack Nicholson, opera singer Vecheclav Osipov, father of wave genetic P. Gariaev, child prodigy Akiane Kramarik, Connie Talbot ... *you can add any creative person you know...*

Table of Contents

Dreams
Translated by Olga Lipovskaya

Amelia Reborn

Egypt

Chapter 1

Amelia Reborn

Amelia Earhart came perhaps before her time... the smiling, confident, capable, yet compassionate human being, is one of which we can all be proud.
(Walter J Boyne.)

Today is April 29th and I had a new past life regression reading. While I was checking my dreams about Atlantis, I suddenly found one dream which occurred 16 years ago and I found another two dreams which connected with this one. I started remembering that these dreams repeated themselves from time to time during my life. In one of the dreams, I saw the same thing at least 5 or 6 times. That's when I decided to visit Di Cherry again to try to understand what it was all about.

It was interesting that on the way to Di Cherry and on the way back, good numbers showed up all the time! They were on each license plate in front of me. Any car near me had a good number; 085, 058. I think something really special happened today, very good and important.

Reading # 4, April 29th 2008

As we started the session, I said to Di, "I come today because I have had this dream a long time ago and I will read it to you now. Since then, I have had a few dreams

7

similar to this one – they kind of continue." I started reading the dream:

Dream # 1
Woman pilot disappeared, dream on June 22, 1992

Time is mixed between past and present. I was dreaming of an old documentary movie, newspapers and this paperboy selling them on the street. In all of these, there is only one subject in all of these newspapers... (Waves of goose bumps go up to my cheeks!) There was a woman, young, maybe 30 or 40 years old. This was before the Second World War. She was wearing a helmet everywhere, like the ones pilots or people in tanks wore. She was always inside in the cockpit of an airplane, operating the controls. I looked at all of this and then I began recognizing it... I recognized everything! I remember it in all of the little details, even feeling and touching the control-panel.

I said to my guide, "This is me!"
"YES, this is you!" he replied.

No one understood what happened to her – she and her airplane disappeared. This goes on for a long time like in a movie. She spoke English and her story was connected to the USA and Canada. I was looking at the screen at first. After I recognized her, and after that, I was inside the cockpit. I touched everything, operated the controls automatically. I know everything without seeing it; it was not necessary for me to see it, I could do this! Half of me was in those times! Lights were burning, flashing, flickering and running.... Everything was real!

I said to Di, "The reason I wanted to do this hypnosis reading is because she is desperate and nobody knows

8

what happened to her. Maybe I carried a heavy emotional luggage in my Spirit. And if we go through this hypnosis session it may be like a treatment, to help me open the door to all these emotions she had when she died or what happened to her, and she could be relieved of the burden, and this won't sit on my Karma – or I don't know how to say this – on my Spirit. This is what I think."

By the way, something very interesting happened when I was at University, there was a boy – a student in our class...

This boy, his name was Oleg, could look at somebody and say something about the person and sometimes he was even rude about it, but what "he predicted" always happened. One time he said to another boy, "Stop eating, you're eating too much; your stomach already needs surgery" or something like that. It was uncomfortable for everybody especially for this boy. This happened around January or February, but when the summer came – I think it was June – this boy went to the hospital to have surgery. He had numerous surgeries. He spent 3 or 4 months in hospital to regain his strength but he was fine in the end.

I remembered the day of the biochemistry exam – the most difficult part of all of what I studied in biology at University – the teacher opened the door, came out in the hallway and invited somebody to come in for the test, and then the next one... and people began running away from the door, because they were afraid. We needed to know all about these molecules, all of these processes – everything in the human body from beginning to end.

I was standing in front of the door and the teacher said, "So you're next?"

"YES, I am next," I replied.

"So you're not running?" the teacher asked.

"NO."

...This student was near me and he suddenly said, "She is not afraid of anything. If you put her in an airplane, she would operate this airplane with her eyes closed. She knows everything about airplanes from beginning to end." It was all very sudden. I looked at him, the teacher looked at him but everybody knew about his strange kind of behavior. So, I just went for the exam and everything was fine, but I remember this moment.

Years later, I was working with the Pratt & Whitney airlines in Los Angeles, CA. They have 1900 Boeings in the Mojave Desert. They have huge airplanes and they have many small aircrafts as well. I was an agent for the airline, trying to seal some deals to buy some of these aircrafts. I remember being very happy there. I would just be running between all of these airplanes, people showing me what the insides looked like. I always ran to the cockpit to see the control panel of each of the planes. All of them were different – especially the small ones. I just loved them! I remember that once I dreamed of buying an airplane – a high-speed jet. In that dream, I ended up owning my own jet and I was so happy!

I said to Di, "Maybe for now we can try to do this. We'll see what happened. The main question we could ask is what happened to her? And maybe we will find an answer. But the main thing for me is that I don't want this heavy emotional burden – if it is still there, I want it to come out."

Di Cherry then put me into a deep hypnosis state and started reading the dream. I always start to envision the dream when she reads it word for word to me – literally how I wrote the dream many years ago. It feels as if some kind of dream-energy is encoded in the words and how they were organized and I start to envision the events when the dream is activated by reading it.

When she finished I started talking:

(Note: The text below is a literal transcription of this session.)

When you read this, I see water in front of me and I see myself in the airplane. We are flying and the sound of this motor is very strong. I hear this sound, my goodness, it is so strong.

When you start saying that it connected with the USA, I see myself with a President, I see a President right near me, and a flag, an American flag and I think...it's inside....

I remember my yellow, yellow... bright yellow airplane, very bright...bright yellow... Canary color. This is Canary color.

Yes. This one I remember, I love this airplane very much, it's my toy.

This being the day, the day of your flight. It's time for you to.... Tell me, are you taking this yellow airplane this time, for your long journey?

No, No, I have another one. I have beautiful airplane, this one best! This one best in the world. I am so proud, this one best airplane. Very beautiful. Very powerful. I am very proud to have it. They make it especially for me, it's

Amelia Reborn? Egypt

for us to fly...Lockheed ...Lockheed... I guess this one much more powerful, much more powerful, and big. I am very proud.

So let's go to the most important event in that life time. See where it takes us. Please go to that most important event in that life time.

I remember my grandmother now and big tree near the house. I remember my grandmother. I love my grandmother. My grandparents I love very much. I remember I am playing near and I have toy, wood toy, you can rolling with little rolls. One like a pig, little pig and another one like a duck, bright colors and I am playing with them. I like to climb to this tree. I remember I like to climb this tree very much. Maybe when I was 8 or 9, I climbed high, too high, my grandmother not happy. She worries that I will fall down.

****

I see myself talking to one club. It's... (Oh, I have goose bumps now! I am covered with goose bumps.) It's club I have and my members in this club and I have meeting. I have meeting for preparation for something and I am talking. It is very happy time, very happy time and I need to go to another city and after to another small city and also talk with people there.

We can go back to your grandmother and the day when you're busy climbing a tree. Just stay inside in that body for a few moments and as you can put her hand in to her arms and you'll find yourself very much smaller, a different shape. I like you to touch with those hands, touch the toys that you just described. How old are you at this time?

Maybe three and half or four, or maybe even three, because I see my hands and they're kind of puffy, like a little kids have. And I touch her hand and she has some bracelet or something. Yes, yes...And I sit on her right leg, on this side....

****

I see myself in some hospital, I am working with some people...like I am doctor or nurse....

Are you a patient there?

No, no I work there and I have this outfit, strange outfit they have those time. They have white apron they have. And this is how they look in those days. Around me nurses... I think I am nurse, I think I am nurse....

****

I see old buildings, bricks buildings, like 3 or 4 floors ... buildings all the same looks, red bricks color. I work in some office; I see office, people coming for help. And I see line. I see line in the hallway.

Line of people or line on the floor?

It's line of people sitting on the chair from this side, from left side. I open door and I invite next one and right now it was mother with two children and she left and now man coming with crutches, this things...he coming inside and we giving to him some papers, I don't know what this... some kind of papers...something....

If you look at those papers, in what language are they written? I'd like you to look at these papers and tell me what you think, in which language they're written?

Amelia Reborn? Egypt

English, all English. I see on the wall English. Beautiful hand writing, people don't make like this hand writing right now. It's beautiful how people write before. No computer by the way in this office. All papers....they are doing something. Across another girl she is writing something. It is lots of papers that time....

****

One man talking to me.... And he makes for me kind of proposal, kind of business proposal. Now he is telling me and it suddenly, strange, unpredictable...what he telling....

He says, "You will just sit, you will just sit, you don't need to operate right now, and you just sit and fly this time."

And I say, "Okay!" I am very proud, I am very, very proud. Something really special, very special....

What does he call you? Does he call you ma'am; does he call you by your first name? Listen, listen to him.

He has voice, bright, kind of low men voice. I like his voice; I like how he talks. He says something... Oh, I have goose bump now so strong like a wave...
He says, "Miss, Miss Amelia you are part of the crew now..." It is so special for me, so special; I am part of team of pilots. I am part, I am passenger, but I am still flying with them....

****

I saw first airplane before...but long time ago.... yes... one on the land... it was some kind of trade show maybe.... That real one was rusty and weird construction... I didn't like it... I lost interest... I lost interest, yes. It kind of strange ... it's something I have long time ago, but I forgot that I want to fly... and now I am flying... and this time it's like a dream come true... I will fly with team of pilots all over the World!

A photographer come and this camera, his camera, he makes crazy flash to the eyes, just crazy flash, right to my eyes. It's hard to keep eyes open, because flash all the time. He asks me to stay near this big motor and he makes pictures right now, I see it.... It is okay to take pictures, but this light killing, just very bright.

After you see something in your eyes you see bright things for sometimes.

Yes, it is true.

Same like you looking to the sun for sometimes...so bright, his camera huge big, heavy....

It is so strange, today, when I am talking, I am using muscles I never used before. I kind of press my nose from both sides. I never did this before in my life, very strange... never used this muscle before... I am pressing my nose like this now, all the time, from time to time.... When I am shy or I worry. I am pressing my nose like this...at the end kind of press it on both side, very interesting; strange for me.... You see it.

It is not easy, when you find yourself in a different body... Yes.

I never knew that these muscles exist, I never use them...but now it is strange....

****

I like name Surinam, Surinam something really special and beautiful.... I was there very short moment...Surinam it is nice name for anything, people or animals...nice Surinam. I like Brazil also, Brazil was nice.... People are very nice. All smiles. I am for them so special. And now we fly and they stay and wave, all of them wave, so many, many people, I see they wave....

****

I am amazed sometimes. I am flying and by the moment I arrive already so many people waiting and so many people waiting and wave to us.... they probably wait for long time, so many people they come....

They support for me, their support, its very important support, because when we flying, it so, so long and its sometimes like forever long... ocean, stars and I know that far away, far, far away hundreds of people waiting for me to come...hundreds of them waiting; they will all come to meet us. It such a big support for me and for Fred... we're very tired... we hardly walk from airplane when we land...our legs can't move... stuck... and... back... we tired so much... so many people waiting....

Yes, they have no idea what you feel like, how tired you are.

Yeah... And I need to look good.... They take pictures...in some places we arrive photographers running.... They take pictures.... We're like people on the war... doing something very serious...and its big responsibility, very big responsibility...for people of America, President and all this newspapers and factory, which give me airplane...big responsibility and we need to be best.... We need to be very good; we're like a hero of some kind...

You are very good.

Because it's long way, very long way...I am glad that I have Fred with me.... When I am flying alone...totally alone... strange feeling. Only when I am fly in airplane I am alone...only those time I think about many, many things in our life...about everything and it very special feeling, because you fly so high.... far from people from everything... and I am think about stars, about future...about past...you kind of think global... about all world ...our Planet so beautiful. Big.
And I remember I work in some hospital...it was war... it was war before...I don't want people to have war, they injured themselves. It happening fast, but healing can take years....and it's painful. I always care about people.

Yes, you do.

I think it is time for me to take you to the day of your death. I count one, two, three... Now!

Through the ocean light. But I scream: "Where we are?" (O, I have now goose bumps so much! Through all my legs goose bumps.) I scream to him...I can not find place, he can not find place. I look all the time, every minute I look to the meter...I want see gasoline, how much left... and it almost zero...it almost zero...and we lost.

We don't see island... we lost! And it's ...its very cold in my head one thing: "This is end, like a robot. This is end, we're lost, no gasoline."
From another side very emotional, very emotional... how can it be now, to finished everything now? Suddenly, cut off. Everything will be cut of, all my promotions; my articles need to be in magazine next month, everything, so many things...so many, many things. It's impossible... it's breaking all plan, we have plan...we fly so long...we should finished this trip...this island right on time, just arrive there.... I think it was mistake in navigation

17

documents, map, which Fred received just before we fly...I think mistake there...

It's unfair, it really unfair...I am doing everything right, but this island just not exists. I don't know where we are...I know this is end. This is end. I see myself ... I watching my own lungs; I pay attention to my lungs. I cannot do nothing. I look to my lung and I know. I know: In my lung wall connected with blood vessels and with air from another side. Inside in the lungs we have air... so when water will be inside and when it touches walls will be no more air; this is moment when I will die. This is moment when I will die.

I only watch.... Can't do anything, impossible to do anything to survive.... This is it. It's last day of my life, Fred life, we will drown now...I think about all kinds of possibility... To swim? We can not swim for long, these sharks will eat us. It better just to be in airplane, in case they will find us, they will bury us ... I am sure they will find us.

I look all the time to the meter and I look to the place where we are. Numbers, numbers, numbers...I look this numbers, I check this numbers. I remember I scream to radio, "We can not see you; we can not see you...." I see these numbers, I remember numbers. I think this is location. This is location. We try going up and down, up and down, we try to find this island, now we go South, more South and straight to east direction. It very strange it should be islands around. But we lost... our flight finished... this is our last point, we arrive here.... Lots of tears, through all this time so many tears, like rivers of tears.... (Long pause.)

(Strange... I am continuing to use this muscle near my nose from both side and top lip... never used them before. Strange....)

And now, it's close, it's within of a moment or two of your death.... And as you go down ... feel it, experience it and breathe ... breathe comfortably, easily ... water in ... water in the cabin ... breathe comfortably and easily... just keep breathing....

(It is interesting even ghosts breathe after they die... they continue, just as humans, to breathe comfortably and easily.... From all deaths, drowning is the best.)

You felt the impact of the plane on the water, it wasn't nice. But you had a good seat. Just allow yourself to go.... It's peaceful. You're leaving through the top of your head; you're leaving that body....

I see inside near this navigation place, some silver metal, square things and there is writing, somebody writes something, like award or just something, it is right there in front of me. Shiny from left side of me, some writing... on the metal, parallelogram shape... maybe a plaque.

Yes, okay. I'd like you to leave your body behind... leave the airplane; it's time for you to trip up, up, up. It is a feeling of being on a child slide, but going backwards. You're leaving behind this beautiful blue planet. The atmosphere looks like a halo around. You're going very, very, quickly. Your guide is there. And look at the number of people who are greeting you! Just as they met you on Earth at all of the places where your plane came down. There are even more people here in Heaven waiting for you, for your company, waiting to welcome you home, to your real life. You've accomplished really what you meant to do. You died at the height of your career. And it was a good trip for us. Very good trip.

Amelia Reborn? Egypt

I see so many people! All like angels. All white kind of, many, many, many.... Door open and I go there.... Yes, they all you can see through, I see them through ... light, light. So many....

****

It was interesting that until the last moment, I continued seeing many people; they all have this see-through kind of looks. If you take, for example, a clear plastic bag and put one inside another maybe 5 or 7 times, this is how it will be, how people look in Heaven. Interesting that in the middle, near the entrance, at the last second, I saw someone like a priest, with the shape of the outfit they wear in the Orthodox or Catholic Churches. He also had the same quality – a see-through being – but with gold color, like gold sand on the upper part....

Wow!!! I visited real Heaven today! I loved it! I didn't want to return from there, by the way. It was such a pleasure to be there, such a light happy feeling!

I think Heaven is only one place for everybody, but for each person the particular space he or she occupies will be according to his or her religion, or in case the person doesn't have any, it will be according to the parents' religion.

I will be more than happy to provide the exact information with the location of the airplane, if it would help finding her aircraft and bury Amelia and Fred's remains, as she hoped to do.

It was very emotional, hard for me to type this last day of Amelia's life during the preparation of the CD. I just can't hear this part again; I am starting to cry.... It feels really unfair that I did not complete that flight to the right place and die there. It didn't finish how it should have done – all of the plans were cut short.

When I flew to Japan, Korea, across the ocean, I knew that if something would happen to the airplane there would be no possibility of survival. I don't like flying over the water; I always preferred flying a different route where there is land beneath me.

Right after the reading, that night, I saw myself again in the airplane, flying over the ocean.... I was Amelia again and I was thinking only about my baby, who was not born yet. Perhaps it was my future baby ... and I started reciting a poem about a little baby! I woke up with this poem on my lips, and with tears in my eyes, I started writing it. This is what I remember:

I am feeling you near,
But where are you?
For many cold years,
I am waiting for you,
My love and my diamond,
My soul and my dream,
I love you forever,
As long as I am here.

Now I understand that Amelia decided to stop flying, simply because deep inside, she still hoped to have a little baby! Sadly it did not happen.... It was interesting that, in my present life, during my post graduation studies, a student predicted that I could die during the birth of my child.   BUT, I wanted to have a child, no matter what! I was ready to die...

Years later, when I was pregnant, I remember that I was hoping to give birth to a baby and at least have the chance to look at my baby's face, hold it in my arms for a second before I would die.... That student was right, it was a life-or-death situation, and GOD supported me in those moments... you know the story. You've been there with me already, right?

Today, November 28, 2008, a letter just arrived with my daughter's birth record. The attending nurse's name was U. Lougheed. The Lockheed Corporation (originally Lougheed_Aircraft Manufacturing Company) was an American aerospace company founded in 1912.

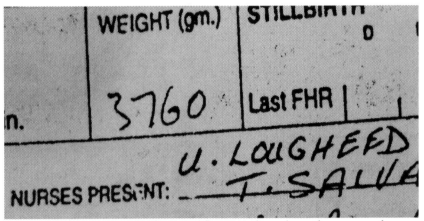

Detail of the Birth Certificate showing the nurse's signature

At the most important moment in my life, during child birth, my Spirit chose a nurse with an airplane name for support! It makes me laugh now....

But now I understand WHY I needed to be a mother in this life. Simply, I needed to complete a wish from my past life. I am glad I did, and now, I have a smart, beautiful daughter.

My friend, Peter, asked me (and I am glad that he asked), "If you were Amelia in a past life, wouldn't you want to be a pilot in this life? Your mind would want to continue with the training and habits it established in a past life.... Yet, in this life, you're not a pilot, not an airplane mechanic."

According to astrology, in our astrological charts we have a North and South node. The South Node represents what we already did very well in our past life, and paying attention to those past goals will interrupt our future development. It is not necessary to continue with past experiences in this present life. The North node, instead, is where we need to go in this life, our goals.

Also, for the Spirit, it is necessary to explore something new, to add quality to what our Spirit already possesses. So, when I was working, for a few years with airplanes, I just collected more information about the progress made in this area. I was hungry to see all of the new airplanes, but after I filled up this 'niche', I lost interest. Same with the medicine books my mother had. I was hungry to read them all – they were huge books – to update my knowledge.

Amelia didn't have children during her lifetime, so she decided to be a mother in this life – no matter what. I can tell you one more of Amelia's secrets; she wished to write more books.... So if you were in Amelia's situation, suddenly dying and thinking that you did not finish or complete something in your life, you would like to know that you will have many lives ahead of you to do it. Well..., today I continue with the book and type the last part of Amelia's life. The reading was difficult for me again. Tears... I prefer never to listen to this CD again. It is very unfair not to complete the flight at the very end, when it was almost done!

It is like a red line around the globe which I can trace with a red marker – all the way around.... But, it did not connect in the South Pacific part.... It stopped there.

Amelia Reborn? Egypt

However, since I lived through all of my past lives and I traveled so much in this present life, I can easily connect this RED line around the globe, even a few times!

So, no more sad thoughts, dear Amelia, because you did not complete that trip around the world, ok? We did it together with the support of your reborn spirit – we were one Spirit.

It goes through Atlantis, Mexico, USA, Egypt, Tibet, Europe, and Canada. And, by the way, this line also connects through the South Pacific, Manihiki Islands, (near the place where Amelia's plane went down) with Hawaii and Los Angeles. I know this for a fact, because I flew this same route for her from New Zealand.

I know why Amelia was lost and why it happened, according to her astrology.

We have 12 houses in astrology. Each represents a different sphere of life. She was a Leo. She was lost one month early, before her birthday. It was July 2; it was under the Cancer sign. For her it was the twelfth house of her horoscope.

Below are some of the meanings for the 12th house:

Mysticism, the occult, psychic matters. Places of seclusion such as hospitals, prisons and institutions. Retreat and reflection and self-sacrifice. Secrets and childhood problems. The subconscious mind, hidden resources, hidden problems, social responsibility. The Twelfth House marks where we may be required to have patience and acceptance, perhaps sacrificing our own personal needs in order to move forward a cause greater than our self. This is where and how we find greater acceptance and the means to embrace fully what life presents to us. [4]

One month before their birthday, people don't have enough energy. It is the end of the energy cycle, which starts from their birth date, each year. Since they have a lack of energy, most people get sick around that time. Yes, Amelia did not feel good before her last flight. I felt it intensely during the hypnosis session; she was sick and very tired during that last flight.

She should have started that flight around the globe at a different time – just one and half to two months later – and everything would have been okay. That way she would have started her flight when her dangerous cycle was finished.

If she had started to remember her past life as a Priest, and chosen the right time according to her astrology, she would have completed her adventure and would have died much later.

I read that statistically 70% of people die during the last month before their birthday – mostly due to health problems. People also get lost easily at that time, no one can find them, or they lose stuff. This is what happened to me when I had a 12th house experience – when I was in Japan. It was September, one month before my birthday. I was totally lost and didn't know how I was going to pay extra for the subway ticket, and finally, I lost control of my stuff, and forgot my bag with all my documents, money, and airplane ticket – everything important was in that bag – and it was stolen.

I remember another 12th house incident, when I went for an audition for a modeling contract. I sat near the door all the time, but they never called me – not until the very end of the audition. I was wondering why they always came out, called somebody else's name and these people did not come for the audition? I asked why, and we found out that my agent had put down a different name for me by mistake.

My business partner, Jay, from California, told me, "A bunch of teens was with my son at my house playing and I couldn't find my digital photo camera." I told him, "It was in July, right?" He was amazed. How did I know this? Simply because I knew that he was born in August.

Once I was lost in China, Beijing. It was September (again a month before my birthday in the 12th house of my horoscope). I went to the park at 5:30 a.m. to see how people study martial arts, Tai Chi and Kung Fu, and lost my way back to the hotel. It was in 1988. At that time, there were only Chinese hieroglyphs around – not one English sign. For almost two hours, I tried talking to people around me in English, trying to find my way back to the hotel.... No luck. I was prepared to live in the street for some time. Then suddenly an old Chinese man asked me, "Can you talk Russian, maybe?" Of course, I can! He showed me to hundreds of people around and said, "No one talks English, but each and everyone here talks Russian. They all studied Russian in school!" Wow! It was a surprise for me! I started laughing at myself!

When people are in the 12th house of their horoscopes, they could also die as a result of an accident. They simply did not see the car approaching or fell down or didn't pay enough attention to what they ate and ended up eating something wrong. Or they take some medicine the wrong way or something else happened to them. My mother and grandmother died a month before their birthdays, the same happened to a few other people whom I was lucky to know during their lifetime. The father of a boy who studied in my daughter's class died because he did not see some electrical wires and was killed. It happened in the last month before his birthday.

My friend, David, died two weeks before his birthday because... (this is really a terrible story, I am not sure if I should put it here, but maybe it will help people to be more careful during the month before their birthday) ...he was at home, in Toronto, with his little granddaughter, Rita, during the 12th house of his horoscope. He simply was not aware of the danger. He did not feel good, so he could not pay enough attention to the little Rita. He allowed her to play on the balcony and she fell down from the 24th floor. She had been trying to see the swimming pool below and bent down too far over the railing. She was a very bright, happy, dancing, and singing child. She, too, was in the 12th house of her horoscope cycle. A few hours later, David himself died of a heart attack. This story is heart-breaking. Yet again, it's good to know that people have many lives and maybe they are re-born already as twins, for example, and will spend a full, long life together. They loved each other deeply during their lives.

In Vancouver we have lots of benches donated by people. You find them everywhere along English Bay and in Stanley Park. I decided to check those statistics and began paying attention to the plaques on the benches. Yes, the statisticians were right! On each bench you can read when the person was born and when he or she died. In most cases the person past away during the last month before his or her birthday! Or they died at the beginning of the month of their birthday, when the cycle ends and they have no more energy left....

Oh no...! My 12-year-old daughter just stepped into my room and told me that she has lost her cell phone....

Amelia Reborn? Egypt

This is June 26 and it is one month before her birthday on July 21 – the 12th house of her horoscope started a few days ago. Well..., what else can I say? I started telling her a week ago that her 12th house would start soon and that she should be careful....

Well..., it was not the end of it. Today, 5th of August, and I have decided to add a few details to this story. After I finished writing this book and my daughter's summer holiday started, we decided to visit the rest of the ancient civilizations on the planet. We flew from Canada via Paris to Rome, visited Greece, Turkey and Crimea.

When we jumped from the train in Rome on July 16th, my daughter suddenly realized that she had forgotten her small backpack, with the camera and our tickets, on the now departing train! The train was on its way to Naples. A few minutes later, we met a handsome Italian journalist, Cristiano, who was pretty tired after two interviews in Milan that day, and who had also forgotten his wallet with money and credit cards on that same train. He was gracious enough to invite us to drive with him to Naples. When we arrived at the station, everything was returned to us instantly – no harm done. But I had to ask – "What month were you born?" That man and my daughter were born just a few days apart – and he belongs to the same astrology sign as she does. That day, when they both lost their stuff, was in the 12th house of their horoscope!

I think it is not necessary to add anything else to this subject in order to support Amelia and explain why she was lost.

I read on a website:
It might appear that whatever happened in the Central Pacific did not fit the pattern of Earhart's previous

problems, but perhaps it did. The fundamental cause of the flight's failure to reach Holland seems to be Earhart's failure to adequately understand the capabilities and limitations of her radio equipment. In other words, she got in over her head, except this time the consequences were not a bent prop and a bruised ego, and this time she couldn't walk away. (http://www.tighar.org/)

I am not agreeing with this, because I know astrology. It was not her ego or whatever people think led her to her death. It was the fact that she was in the 12th house of her horoscope! Yes, Amelia was not fully aware of the capabilities and limitations of her radio equipment, because she was in the 12th house of her horoscope at that moment, which closed all possibility for her to understand how serious the situation was. This is the same thing that happened to David and Rita. Amelia tried her best and she was very organized. It was NOT her ego. (I am angry because of the last sentence in that paragraph in that website.)

Knowledge of astrology is a powerful thing. Why did President Reagan meet with Gorbachev in Reykjavik in the middle of the ocean with such good results? Because his astrologer advised him to do it that way. Why was the Declaration of Independence (marking the birth of the USA) signed in the middle of the night? According to astrology, time and place to do something are very important. I am sure if we asked a professional astrologer why Amelia was lost at that particular time and place, s/he would give us a serious explanation.

As you know, after reading the chapter about The Priest, I am acting in my daily life like a priest for a few months now. I am learning some new things, which I love and I am studying from him, or I start remembering things from my past life and continue to cultivate them, trying to develop them.

It is interesting that the same happened after the reading about my past life as Amelia.

During the hypnosis session, I developed new habits; I started using muscles I never used before! I always press my nostrils together, for example. The next day, I walked down the street and noticed that I walked differently! First, I tried to be taller, straightening my back, (Amelia was taller than me). Second, I walked with bigger steps, making wider movements with my arms, and pointed ahead of me with the three forefingers of my hand. Now, if someone asks me how the Priest walked and how Amelia walked I can show them and people see the difference instantly.

Searching for Amelia

A few hours after the reading, I found out, on the internet, who Amelia was and that her airplane is still missing. I called the company which tried to find her and which was preparing for their second voyage. I told the director that I just found out that I was Amelia in my past life, that I knew the location of the airplane and that I wished to divulge it to him. I told him that I am very happy about their efforts in trying to find her aircraft and that I am ready to help as much as I could. If they wanted, I said, I could even fly with them to the place and invest my feelings into this, which would point us and navigate us in the right direction. It was nice to hear that they already had a plan where to search this time, "but please also check the location I have," I said. "Because the location I got through the hypnosis session is near the Kiribati Republic! I can tell you the exact place!" I also mentioned that with the goose bump sensation I experienced this spring, while visiting places where I was in my past lives; maybe, they could monitor my skin reaction to give them direction and help navigate the search.

The problem was that he simply didn't believe that it could be possible; that people have many lives and he couldn't see any value in past life regression. Me too! I was exactly the same just five months ago. I didn't believe it. I am a scientist. I didn't even want to go to any of these sessions. I told him about my experience and proposed to put me into a deep hypnosis state with some specialists of his choosing to ask Amelia directly, one more time, the exact location of her aircraft: "Where is the airplane right now?" He didn't want to do the session, even with his own hypnosis specialists. He had nothing to lose – he could only gain popularity when he would finally solve the mystery, right?

Now it looks like his organization has plans to search for Amelia's aircraft on Nikumaroro Island, Phoenix Islands, southwest of Hawaii, and near the Kiribati Republic where they found a shoe and a little aluminum engine part.[1] I am sure he is a professional and he

---

[1]   I saw in http://www.tighar.org/TTracks/14_2/14-2Bones.html that bones were found in the Nikumaroro Islands in 1938 by a British colonial administrator of Irish descent, Gerald B. Gallagher, whose nickname was in fact, "Irish."
"When only about 24 hours out of Suva, he died. The natives are superstitious as the devil and the next night ... they threw the gunnysack full of bones overboard".   Actually this person: *"Gallagher did not die in a boat 24 hours out of Fiji, but he did die on Nikumaroro about 24 hours after returning from leave in Fiji."* So he did bring bones to Fiji for forensic examination. This incident with its CURSE can be one of the extra proofs that these were Amelia's bones! YES, it sounds weird, but this is exactly what it is! Hers and my past lives were Ancient Maya Priest and Egyptian Royal Priestess. The Spirit was angry with this man, Gerald. I guess it was not in the Spirit's plan for bones to be found so soon. Thomas E Devine wrote a number of books saying that Amelia was killed by Japanese on Saipan and he died. R. Wallack pretends that he saw her briefcase on

31

knows very well what he is doing. I wish them lots of luck!

So, I just went for a tomato juice refill and started playing my Priest's rock from Mexico. Believe me, perhaps more than anyone on the planet, I wish to find her airplane, solve the mystery and bury the bones of my previous life! Maybe this is one of the reasons why I was re-born. It is strange that this man dedicated maybe all of his life in the search for Amelia's airplane; that he made a wonderful website with Amelia's biography, but that he did not want to deal with the person who was the real Amelia in her past life.

I just laughed when he closed his eyes trying to avoid seeing the real person. Maybe he is afraid of ghosts? I told him, in passing, that I was not a ghost, but, YES, I could understand his point of view, too.

Saipan and died from throat cancer. He was cursed as well. There was NO Japanese around. Only bones of native people were found on that island. It is a shame that people play games around Amelia's death. During my present life, people around me have lots of luck, gain prosperity, and some win the lottery, but 6 were punished! They were CURSED in some strange way when they did something really bad for people or community around them! Usually people broke bones and time was given to them to be alone at home, to think, to re-examine their lives and attitude. When it happened a few times, I started to warn people, asking them to stop..., trying to prevent the next outcome. (For example once, the hospital called a young scientist, my friend, asking her to come URGENTLY. Her grandfather was dying. It was around 11 a.m. But our boss didn't let her go until the end of the day. Her grandfather died alone, because the rest of the family was in another country, her father worked as an Ambassador. That bad boss broke his hand the next morning...)
Thank you to all the team at www.tighar for your great job searching for Amelia and her airplane.

This subject dealing with past lives is unusual and strange. I chose to share my information with him, because I deeply appreciated his work and his enormous effort in the search. I am sure, if I made it my goal, I could collect funds without his organization and find Amelia and Fred's remains, bury them and bring that airplane to the museum.

But when I try to imagine how I would start asking people to donate money in order to bury bones from my past life ... it makes me laugh.... It sounds funny! We will survive with Amelia without that, I am sure. But that aircraft... I wish to find it and lift it from the ocean.... It is still in my mind like a dream toy. I have this enormous attachment to that airplane, deep in my heart and Spirit. I think if Amelia loved airplanes so much it is a great honor for her to have it as a coffin.

I wish that, when I die to have an epitaph on my tombstone that reads: "Here lies to rest the last reincarnation of the Spirit of the Mexican Priest Jaguar, the Pilot, Amelia from USA, and the woman from the Atlantis kingdom...." What a team! I imagine what it would be like if they were alive and together, they would be like twins – triplets actually – different on the outside but exactly the same on the inside.

Nostradamus wrote 3 quatrains about Amelia Earhart. You can find their interpretation in The Strange Disappearance of Amelia Earhart, Nostradamus and the New Prophecy Almanacs Michael McClellan. www.newprophecy.net/pastceleb.htm [11]

Quatrain 10.84
The natural girl so high, high, not low,
The late return will bring grief to the contented,
The long journey will not be without debates
In employing and losing all of her life.

Quatrain 2.45
Too much the heavens weep at the birth of Androgyn,
Near the heavens human blood is spilled:
Through death too late a great people renewed,
Late and soon comes the awaited assistance.

On that website discussions refer to the reasons Nostradamus called Amelia an Androgyn.

I think Nostradamus wished to point out that Amelia was doing a man's job. She was a leader of the feminist movement, and she was wearing men's clothes: leather jacket, pants. She was extremely brave, concentrated on her goal with persistence, which helped her to fly solo across the world. Maybe Nostradamus also felt that Amelia was a Priest, in her past life and that she carried this man's quality: "tomboy", hunting?

Michael McClellan: *Still, line 3 Quatrain 2.45 remains a mystery. Through death too late a great people renewed, its meaning does not seem applicable to Earhart's final adventure, raising the possibility that this quatrain may be a repetitive one. Thus, we see both the Amelia Earhart of the past and a futuristic entity, yet to be conceived or created perhaps, who will truly be biologically sexless.*

It makes me smile.... I am here called a "futuristic entity", which will truly be biologically sexless. I should tell Michael McClellan that I am reborn and I am a mother in this life and a normal woman, not an Androgyn and, by the way, people think that I am pretty feminine and sexy. So Amelia was a normal woman as well, not an Androgyn, such as people described her in this article. It is important to understand that the Spirit is built as a hologram – a multi-layered structure. This unique crystal, which everyone has, collects memory of both characteristics: male and female, and all of the past lives they had. In Amelia's case it included the Priest and now this Spirit is added to all of my characteristics as well.

So, when Nostradamus said, "Through death too late a great people renewed," he talked about re-incarnation and here I am, Amelia re-born!

The concept of androgyny was further developed by the feminist movement, which emphasized that human personality is made up of both masculine and feminine characteristics. If males develop their 'feminine' side, and females their 'male' side, it was argued, differences could be lessened, and rigid stereotyping avoided.
Androgyn – Hutchinson encyclopedia, article about Androgyn

A Three-Spirit Connection

I arrived a few days ago from Egypt and I am still on European time, now in Canada. I woke up at 3:15 a.m. this morning and started working on the book. I have been typing for the last 16 hours – it is now 7:20 p.m. – already. I only took a few short trips to the kitchen to refill my glass of tomato juice. Usually 1.89 liter last me for the day until the next morning. I prefer the Extra Spicy Tomato-Clam cocktail, which is a "Safeway" brand, when I am working on the computer. Since I can't drink coffee or real tea, the spices in this juice keep me in great shape to type for a long time and ... I didn't fall asleep while flying my airplane in my past life.....

My daughter asked me a few days ago: "Why you always in this pilot shirt at home, when you have so many beautiful things to wear?"
Interesting... I had never paid attention to this; that I typed all this book often wearing a T-shirt with a map of

the Caribbean Islands (the Atlantis place – I prefer T-shirts with maps) underneath my favorite shirt. I looked down at this khaki, light green color shirt and wow! She was right! It is a pilot shirt, from L'Aero-Club de France, "Flying with the best" and with the logo of a small propeller airplane on the front pocket... I think I know why I was deeply attached to this shirt for the last 10 years.... I wish to have Amelia's "99 Club" shirt one day, if they still exist. No doubt I would live in those shirts 24/7....

It is interesting that I did X-ray studies with seeds. X-rays came from my living in Atlantis and my interest in the seeds, I guess, came to me from the Priest and Amelia's sides...?

It is also interesting to note that the town where Amelia was born, Atchison, is the "Most Ghostly Town" in USA. Probably, there is some special electromagnetic field surrounding the area.[2] This makes me think that perhaps the Priest was close to these Spirits subjects during his life and it attracted Amelia to be born in such a place as well. I know for sure that the Priest was the one who passed onto Amelia and me the same love for hunting, biology, plants and healing the sick.

My whole room is painted white, with white corals, white sand from the Caribbean and the South Pacific, with the white, big, musical limestone from Mexico, the limestone pyramid, a souvenir from Chichen Itza and the white limestone pyramid from Giza, Egypt. The furniture is white with gold trimming, and many turquoise-color accessories accent the décor – a huge painting with the ocean of turquoise water (the same as Atlantis, in the Caribbean), and another painting with turquoise colors. My bedding set, my robe, and many of

---

[2] Amelia Earhart often spent her holidays in Kirwin, a <u>Mining Ghost Town</u> in Colorado with her husband, George Putnam and asked to build a cabin for her nearby.

my outfits are turquoise. The entire room is decorated in white and turquoise, like a white sand beach with the turquoise water of the Caribbean, or Atlantis and Mexico. It looks like I used to live in white palaces in Atlantis, and in white carved buildings in Chichen Itza and it had an influence on my current environment and that for many years, for as long as I can remember, in fact.

Some time ago, my daughter asked what I was doing; what kind of book was I writing? So I gave the first few pages of the book about the Priest for her to read. She returned to me and asked, "How long did you sleep with Sweetheart and turtle?"

10 years ago, at the age of two, she got two very nice cat-toys that looked almost real – one black and one white. The white one, which she named Sweetheart, she gave to me. Ever since then, I sleep hugging the big white cat every night. For Christmas, I got a sea turtle and now I sleep with my right hand on her soft, velvet smooth shell. And now, here is my daughter pointing out that the Priest had a white jaguar and a turtle and that I am sleeping with a white cat and a turtle! Well..., I had not notice this until today. It is amazing how many things follow us from one past life to another.[3]

Who is Amelia?

That day, after the reading, I returned home and decided to Google: *Amelia, pilot woman* and *Fred, Pilot, disappeared.*

I was hoping that maybe something would come up.

---

[3] You will find a list of the common traits in life, their characters, habits, looks, interests, and activities between Amelia, the Priest, the Queen of Atlantis and Julia Svadihatra in the Table of Common Characteristics at the end of the book.

Amelia Reborn? Egypt

To my big surprise, there are many articles on the internet with Amelia Earhart's name. [4]

As soon as I saw her photos, I recognized her instantly – the same woman I saw in my dream, in those long documentary movies and on the front-page of all of these old newspapers, which the paperboy was selling! I had goose bumps again, and each time I saw them. I knew everything there; I recognized all of these airplanes. I remembered the car on the photo, everything inside the car, the spacious interior, the high seating and the low front window. Fred looked very familiar to me also; it felt as if I knew how he talked, his voice, and how he walked, how he laughed.

Wow! I started reading about her and I was amazed how many similarities there are between the two of us. Yet, there was something even more amazing to me about her; she had so much in common with the Priest from Chichen Itza! I wondered if she had a déjà-vu feeling

---

4　With purpose, I avoided watching documentary movies about Amelia or read anything about her, because I tried to make direct contact with her and acquire information as to how I felt about her through the hypnosis sessions and my dreams. The book was finished when I allowed myself to look through this information. As soon as I watched the first movie, I saw that Amelia wrote: *"The stars seemed near enough to touch and never before have I seen so many."* Now I know why I ran with little kids trying to touch the STARS!
I also just found out in the same movie that not only the Priest exercised in the Ball Court, but Amelia played BASKETBALL as well!
Wow! I did not exercise or play basketball, but this skill, which they both developed and gave to me as an inheritance, helped me to "survive" when I tried to avoid gymnastics in school and instead threw balls into the hoop without mistakes, precisely, and gained good points this way. (See The Priest chapter.)
Amelia was very good in MATH; I also finished special math school. This helped me understand multidimensional world much easier. (See Violet field chapter.)

while she visited Mexico. It is three people – three lives of one Spirit. Yes, all of them had the same consciousness, thoughts and actions.

I am lucky that I can compare the Priest's life and mine, with Amelia's life, because so many facts about her life are available on the internet. It helps me and my readers understand the way one Spirit continues his life through the centuries and exists in the next and the next human life.[5]

From my past life as Amelia Earhart, the pilot, I have similar interest for music, poetry, biology, zoology,

---

[5] One person sent me letters regarding
http://www.ameliareborn.com/ and mentioned the website
http://www.irene-amelia.com/
Interesting! I found out that *"Amelia Earhart was a known devout pacifist, was a 'world humanitarian. She was also deeply spiritual, an artistic thinker, and she commanded a supreme intellectual quality. She also very much adored the cultures of the Orient, and the social and religious philosophies inherent to the countries of China and Japan".*
This is exactly the description of who I am now in this life! I am against war and violence. I just can't watch movies about war or violence.
I visited Japan, China and South Korea during the last 18 years at least 20 times and was even told by a Highest Monk that one of my past lives was spent in Asia. It looks like this is the reason why Amelia and I were attracted to Asia. *"As well, she always had trouble with limelight living, and a marriage prone to expect almost anything but true love from her person."* I had marriage proposals from famous people, celebrities and rich tycoons during the last few years, since I am single again, but true love is the most important factor for me. I wrote that Amelia was a *"Worker in charge of children ranging from toddlers to teens"* This is what I saw during the hypnosis sessions, when a mother comes to Amelia in some office with 2 children!
By the way, it is impossible – NO WAY – that Amelia was kidnapped or immigrated to Japan under somebody's name. Please read the book and the hypnosis sessions. It is not her, and my character is not to hide and run. What reason would she have to do this?

chemistry, physics, fine arts, drawing, clothes design, modeling and aviation, in this life.

Sciences

I finished university with a teaching degree in biology and chemistry. I was top-of-the-class in physics and graduated with honors. I was the only one, from hundreds of students, who got a "RED diploma" (meaning I was the best) that year. After that, I took post-graduate courses in horticultural physiology, biochemistry, and X-ray. Since I was five years old, I had a private teacher who taught me how to play the piano. At the age of six, I began attending ballet classes. From the age of seven, and for the next seven years I went to music school. I enjoy studying music and the biography of the famous classical composers. My favorite music, which I loved to play, was Mozart's bright and happy music and that of the wise John Sebastian Bach.

My essays in poetry and stories were the best in school. Our principal collected them and read them to the pupils in my class, and continued to do this even after I left school.

When it was time to go to university I tried to decide whether I wanted to be a doctor like my mother or study plants to be a scientist like my father. I wish to be a doctor and a scientist at the same time. By the age of 14, I had read all of the medicine books my mother had in the house. They were big, heavy books, encyclopedias about internal medicine, microbiology, gynecology, skin disease, biochemistry and so on and so on. I loved it and it was like a food for me, to which I was addicted. It was impossible for me to stop devouring the knowledge contained in these books – until I would come to the end of each one. I guess I chose my parents before I was born. I decided to study plants only because I worried that I would make a mistake as a doctor.

Amelia loved biology, science and spent lots of time with medicine, working in hospitals and studying. I have a state-of-the-art diagnostic machine and I am checking everyone's health trying to help my friends – I do this as a hobby.

Science Fiction and Fine Arts

By the way, I read them all; I mean every book we had in our school library.
My aunt, Merry, always sent me science fiction books; I read them during math classes, because I always had time to read after I finished the assignments quickly. More than once, our math teacher took the book I was reading and punished me by withholding the book until the end of the year. In the end, she had a good collection of science fiction books, maybe around 12 or 14 of them.

I loved books about fine arts. I can stare at paintings for hours. I loved to visit the Hermitage and spent days there, and I am planning to visit the Louvre in Paris this summer. I always envy the people who live in St. Petersburg. They can go any day and see the many paintings displayed in the museums! You can see examples of my own drawings in this book. Thanks to Amelia; I gained from her, as an inheritance, her drawing skills, which she developed during her life.

Airplanes and Aviation

I have a time-tested friend (or a longtime friend) in Japan. Gousaku Michihata is his name and he is a retired Major General of JASDF (Japanese Air Self-

Defense Force). He had worked as an experimental test-pilot for many years to put new aircrafts through their test-flights, and in the training of test-pilot students. "Experiment" meant no one was privy to the results of the tests, which included whether the prototype aircrafts would fly or would land safely.

It was funny; when I asked him, "What month, what day were you born?" He replied that he was born on October 8th.
"8th of October?" I asked.
"Yes, October 8th," he repeated.

I thought that maybe he did not understand English very well and I repeated what I said. We were born on the same day, and month, and almost at the same place!

Mr. Gousaku Michihata in the cockpit of an F-4EJ
Phantom before take-off

Gousaku Michihata beside F-104J
Starfighter after landing

He gave me good advices about airplanes. I wondered if he was Fred Noonan in his past life.

For some unexplained reason, I flew to the middle of the South Pacific to a tiny island and started working there with some black pearl farmers. It is a 12-hour flight from Los Angeles to the Cook Islands, followed by a four-hour flight in a small-prop over the ocean to Manihiki Island.

43

(From left) Julia, a pearl farmer and Michihata in Tokyo

Now, six years later, I know exactly what attracted me to that place. Manihiki Island is located in the middle of the South Pacific Ocean very close to the place where Amelia's aircraft disappeared.

Mr. Michihata Gousaky started working with me as an agent, representing the black pearls trade in Japan. Our company participated often in the jewelry trade shows. Once, I brought a couple of real pearl farmers from Manihiki Island to Tokyo, to the trade show, to teach them the business. Everyone ran to meet the "real pearl farmers" – magazines and newspapers reporters included. Usually, in this lucrative business, pearls are going through the hands of six or more people before they end up in the stores in Japan.

I worked with airlines – with the department of United Technology and with Pratt & Whitney Company in 2004. When they showed us a warehouse full of huge parts of airplanes, and engines, I was extremely excited and experienced the most astonishing, happy feeling – something I never felt.

In the Mojave Desert, in California, I just ran between hundreds of Boeings and all kinds of small airplanes. I was hungry to see what was inside them all. What was in each of the cockpits? Wow! What a huge, shiny engine! This cutest, private, luxury jet was such a great toy! It felt as if my dream had come true. It felt as if I had dreamed about it a long time ago – many years ago...

Mojave Desert, California, 2004

What a luxury "toy"!

Jaguar outfit, airport map, California, 2004

In this photo we are discussing the plans for the reconstruction of the airport. As you can see, for such an important meeting, I covered myself in Jaguar print.

Unbeknownst to me then, the Priest and Amelia were supporting me in those days!

The Business Plan – an unfolded accordion

It was interesting that the business plan for the airline was prepared on a long sheet of paper – opening up like an accordion. I was so excited to see it that I even took a photo of it.

The Priest had a big book, pages of which opened exactly in the same way – as an accordion!

See, here again two things – the business plan about airplanes (Amelia's connection), and the Priest's book (the accordion).

By the way, the man on the right of the photograph is a legendary man. Somehow, I meet "extreme" people way too often. He is the only man, in recorded history, who survived a fall from an aircraft from a height of 1500 meters. At the time, he was responsible for the training of cosmonauts in critical situation as part of the Space Program in Russia. He was training over the Black Sea, when suddenly, his airplane experienced some malfunctions and it started spinning down. Everyone on board parachuted to safety, but since he was the head of the mission, he left the plane last, and his parachute did not open! This brave man was, at that time, teaching how to survive a fall from great heights – he taught me as well. What saved his life was the fact that he went down into the water keeping his legs straight, so there was the least surface of impact – he hit the water with the soles of his feet. Nevertheless, he suffered two broken legs; some ribs were fractured as well, and so on. But, now, years later, he is active and has almost fully recovered. When we were in Disney Land after the meeting, I noticed that it was hard for him to stand for a long time to watch the parade. His name is George Nazarenko. In Ukrainian, Nazarenko means "from SUNRISE". He is the owner of a private airline in Russia and he celebrates his second, re-born life each year and he counts each coming year as a gift from God, who helped him stay alive. I am sure that our meeting in this lifetime was not an accident. After all, I know that, in my past life as Amelia, my airplane also fell into the water... so we understand each other on some other level, pretty well, and I help his airline, as an agent, as much as I can.

I also was ready to move to Brazil to start selling the Embraer in the summer of 2005. I adore my cousin, who works as a new aircraft builder in Russia. I was very happy to see, touch, and check all sorts of airplanes during the 2005 MAX Show in Moscow!

MAX Air Trade Show in Moscow, 2005

I visited the South Pacific many times – Cook Islands and Manihiki Island, which is close to the place where Amelia Earhart disappeared. It looks like my Spirit tries to attract me to the place where my past life ended.[6]

---

6   Amelia had a dress with a big white collar and loved it! I had exactly the same dress with a big white collar; it had been designed by the famous Vecheslav Zaizev for an important business trip to China to sign an agreement. I drew this collar

I was modeling and working in that area: in Hawaii and Pacific islands. It is a heavenly, beautiful island in the South Pacific where pure white sandy beaches are full of amazing white corrals. The turquoise water is full of bright multicolored, tropical fish, and in the jungle, you can find blossoms, rare orchids with gardenias spreading wonderful fragrance around. People are wearing flowers and leis in their hair every day. When I was sitting for the first time on the white, sandy beach, between white corrals, I was thinking, "If ever Heaven exists on Earth it is here". I did not know then that my past life ended there and I went to Heaven exactly from this place.

Kauai, Hawaii 2007 – photo by Tim Orden

and asked him to make the dress with it. Now my favorite top by Victoria's secret also has this big white collar. I designed all of my dresses and even three dresses for the "Avon" company.

It is interesting that the owner of the place, where I stayed on Cook Islands, was named "Aunty NOO". It was the name of the navigator who was with Amelia, when the airplane disappeared – his name was Fred *Noo*nan. It is also interesting to note that Fred was born in Cook County (Chicago).

In a past life, I was *Amelia*. This is the name of a beautiful flower – the big Lily kind. The Lily is my favorite flower. I always wish to have a flower name. I picked the name Jasmine Rose for myself and I have been using it everywhere since 2000. And I still wish to change my name for Jasmine Rose Lily! It sounds funny, too many flowers, right? But this is what I really want.

Modeling for a label of herbal products from Scotland
(Photo by Stefan Wunderli)

Amelia Reborn? Egypt

I always love overalls and all kinds of clothes with many pockets, to put all kinds of stuff in them, like instruments or tools. I saw a photo of Amelia in a brown, leather overall and instantly remembered that I bought a long, leather, brown coat when it came in fashion (at a sky-rocketing price) of exactly the same color and quality! I remember my reaction when I saw it; I just wanted it – right there and then – I didn't think twice about buying it.

When I was small, I loved the children's fairytale entitled "The Magician of the Emerald town" (or "The Wizard of Oz"). According to the story they lived in a city named Kansas. Each time when my parents read me this story my heart melted.... What a magic place it was, this Kansas! It was my dream town. Before I went to sleep, I often thought about this town, trying to imagine what it looked like. I never knew that this was a real place until I moved to Canada. I wished to visit this city as soon as I could, but it is too far away from Vancouver and the only slim excuse I had to go there was the fairy-tale. Now I found out that Amelia was born in Kansas! My past life was there and this explains my deep attachment to the place. I still wish to visit Kansas someday and I wonder what I will experience in this place. Will it be the same as to what I experienced in Mexico in Chichen Itza and in Egypt?

Perhaps the reason I moved away from Europe was that I lived in North America as an Atlantis woman, as a Priest from Mexico and as Amelia from the USA in my three past lives.

I remember a few years ago I saw a story on TV about reincarnation. It was about a little girl in India. From an early age she began to tell her parents that she lived before in a town nearby and that she was married and that her husband, a doctor, had an affair with his nurse and they killed her and dropped her near a railway, near some river. Her parents decided to go to that city and check her story. They made a documentary movie and showed how they arrived with their car to that city, how this girl pointed to the parents' house and her previous parents waiting for them on the balcony. She ran inside the house and showed everyone where her toys and books were – which her past-life father had kept for some reason. It is the only case in history where a person, her husband, from her previous life was charged and is now in jail!

While I am writing this book, I am thinking about all of these re-born situations and always come back to one question, which has been in my mind for years. Are people who died, often re-born in the same family or in a nearby place? Yes. I got this positive answer from a few different sources.

My mother died from sickness at the age of 59 – way too early and suddenly. She came in my dream three months after her death. She stood in front of me and smiled. I don't know why but I asked her, "Maybe it is time to be re-born?"

She continued to smile, didn't say anything. Kind of, "I don't know.... I will think about it...." Soon after that, I was pregnant – at the most uncomfortable moment of my modeling career, when I got a very lucrative contract!

As soon as the child started to walk and talk everything she did reminded me of my mother. First, she wanted to be a doctor, like my mother was, since she was two years old. She was always wearing a doctor's hat with a cross and a white lab-coat which I made for her. She drew cats with a doctor's hat in a situation where another cat visits the doctor.

Patient visiting the Doctor with the cross on the hat

The first time we visited my mother's sister, my aunt, Merry, when my daughter was 2.5 years old, she found many of my aunt's necklaces on the dresser. She was particularly attracted to the white pearl necklace and put it around her neck immediately.

I asked her to give it back, worried that she would break it and all the pearls would fall everywhere on the floor. (This is what a little baby does usually.) But she didn't want to give it back! She repeated, "This is mine! This is mine! This is mine!" Years before, I had brought to my mother and my aunt exactly the same pearl necklace from China.

Is this 'baby' my mother reborn?

Secondly, she suddenly started asking about her potty! She stopped using it a long time ago already, in Canada! Since my aunt never had any children of her own, there was no way she would have one. But my daughter was adamant: "Give me my potty!"

Finally, my aunt heard that we were fighting and came to the living room. She told me that there was no need to fuss about this, that she indeed had a potty! And she brought a brand new one out of the cupboard. I was very surprised and asked my aunt, "Why have you got a potty? For what?"

She then told me that my mother brought this potty to my grandmother one day and after she died, when my grandmother moved to my aunt's place, to another city, the movers put this potty with everything else. I was even more surprised then. I asked, "Why did mother buy this potty in the first place?"

My grandmother said that my mother told her that she was walking once in the street and saw people selling it, and she started to think that maybe one day she would need it, and she bought it! Well, she was a doctor, maybe she was thinking that one day she would be very sick in bed and would need a potty. Anyway, my daughter got what she was asking for and she was very happy! She played with it for the next few days.

Two days later we arrived at my father's home, in another city.
My father remarried another woman after my mother died. We went to visit him and his new wife then, and we stayed there for five days. During all this time my child did not eat any food there! My daughter refused to touch anything that his new wife brought her on a tray to her room. She would take the tray and throw it out into the hallway and shut the door of the room! This behavior was unexplained. I was very worried. She was hungry and I had to change our tickets to fly home earlier than anticipated. All this baby ate, during the five days we were there, were cookies which my aunt had made and which she gave to her in a big bag. If she is my mother reborn maybe she couldn't forgive my father for re-marrying so soon after she passed away? Or perhaps she was jealous of this other woman?

But the next thing that happened really made me think that she was my mother in her past life. One morning she closed the door of her bedroom (where she used to live) from the inside. My father and his wife were very worried. I didn't understand why. They told me that a child would never be able to open this door and it may be necessary to call a locksmith and break it down in order to open it!

My father said that only my mother knew how to close this door from inside the room. He tried to close it many times – to no avail. We then all started asking the baby to open the door but she ignored us and continued to play. Suddenly, when we were about to call the locksmith, she ran to the door and opened it without any problems!

The next day we needed to fly home but my father had organized a farewell party for that evening. The guests were having a good time when a young man, who had visibly too much to drink, started following me. So I went to another room to sleep. I tried to close that door for at least half an hour, worried that the man would follow me and wake me up and the baby! And I couldn't close this damn door! I tried everything possible.... So I ended up sitting in the chair, shut off the light near the baby and waited until all the guests had left.

I have a list of the common things between my mother and my daughter ... not genetic ones, by the way.

Maybe this girl is the result of my unique capability to talk/deal with dead people, direct them to another world and guide them to do things I want them to do. Is this my heritage from the Priest? My daughter ... is my mother?

The case below is absolutely amazing! I read about it in a newspaper, it filled two pages, (no kidding!). Sadly I gave this article to my friends to read, they gave it to someone else and those people moved and lost it! Everybody in this story are real people, with their names, last names, photos and many details regarding the places they were born, worked and so on.

Here is the story:
During the Second World War a boy and a girl were in the Russian army. They deeply love each other and were always together for four years. At the very end of the war, the blond girl was killed. The war ended. The broken-hearted boy returned to Leningrad and continued to work at the factory, where he worked before the war started.

A few years later, in a small Russian town, a young boy and a girl were on a scooter and had an accident. The boy died as a result, and the girl was in a coma for a month. When she woke up from her coma she did not recognize anyone from her life. No one. She only talked about the war, about some man she loved and missed, and she wished to find him. She cut her hair, adopted a different hairstyle and colored it blond. She arrived at the factory in Leningrad where the man worked. He said that she was taller and looked different than the other girl he loved and lost. But everything else was exactly the same! How she talked, how she laughed, all of her habits and so on were the same. Only she and he knew many things which no one else knew. They got married, had a daughter and spent 20 happy years together until she died as a result of the onset of complications after the motorcycle accident. A group of Russian scientists studied and monitored her case until she passed away. They proved absolutely that this girl is the same one which died during the Second World War. However, they could not explain how it could have been possible.

I guess the Spirit of the first girl wished to return to her boyfriend, the man she loved and perhaps made a deal with the Spirit of the girl which was in the scooter accident, or most likely, it just took over her body without asking her. But I think it happened with God's help and his personal approval. The power of love was stronger than death and won this game!

Back to Amelia

Here are some the habits, which we have in common: (Richard E. Gillespie, Amelia Earhart. http://www.tighar.org/Projects/Earhart/ResearchPape rs/Earhart.html#2

Amelia does not drink coffee or tea, she takes tomato juice instead.
I can't drink tea, especially dark or strong, for as far as I can remember. I drink herbal tea sometimes – always very light. And I just cannot drink coffee.

She loved tomato juice.
I love and drink tomato juice every single day with all kinds of spices. My grandmother knew about my love for tomato juice. For many years in the fall she used to buy boxes of tomatoes and made juice, and some with little tomatoes inside it. I remember the three- and five-liter-jars at her place. She had tomato juice ready for me all-year-round.

It is strange but for some reason, I just can't drink tea. Everybody in my family drinks all kinds of teas. So it is not genetic. I was wondering, how come with my perfect health, I have a problem with this. When I read that Amelia also did not drink tea, I was very surprised. Our bodies, hers and mine, can't accept tea! Please tell me how it could be possible that this characteristic transferred with the Spirit into a new body? I even decided to check one more time and I agreed to drink one cup of tea with my aunt Merry, during my visit this summer. I felt so, so bad, I lost a whole day because I couldn't do anything with this terrible, sickening feeling. I counted the hours, waiting for my body to get rid of it. But as a scientist, I decided to check one more time and drank another cup today! At the last moment, I got scared and mixed the one cup of tea with one glass of pure water. Unfortunately I got the same really bad result! It was 9:00 a.m. when I drank my "test potion" and I felt awkward until 7:00 p.m. Another entire day lost! I wonder what else was wrong with Amelia, what kind of health or allergy problems she had and checked if I have the same. I am lucky that I can compare my life with my previous life, because of Amelia's popularity.

****

I think the Spirit body looks like a 3-D hologram, with some sort of crystal-like appearance. For some reason, I always see my Spirit as a perfect, strong crystal, as perfect as a diamond.

Our body is covered with an energy field, which is actually a matrix, a plan of the body structure. Inside our body there are over a million biochemical changes occurring every second. Our body is in constant changes. This plan around the body controls its functions and re-builds everything according to that plan. Maybe this energy field structure is responsible for our thinking process and consciousness. The thinking brain can only exist on biochemical or at the molecular and atom levels, where the possibility of "containers" for the consciousness on the level of elemental particles and their fields may exist. The Biofield is an ideal environment for *fluctuation*, which are holograms. It is possible to say that the biofield is actually a multi-component hologram. This way all of the person's life experiences – all his words, thoughts, words he ever said or someone said to him, what he saw, what he felt, all of his emotions – everything is preserved in that biofield in the form of holograms. These sets of holograms together form a kind of crystal, which we could name Soul or Spirit.[7] [10]

In addition, I am sure the crystals' structure of the Spirit is the best to collect and save information from one lifetime to the next.
The same as with any kind of information, to preserve it on the real crystals is much better than using something like CDs, DVDs or paper.

I am thinking now that when people travel through the Universe in their dreams, what we call here, an "astral body" is actually this crystal made from sets of many hologram components. It is interesting that the body of the person, who left with visitors from another planet to see their world, did not exist in time and space. Maybe it is transformed into the field structure, because this is the only way of entering the world of the field forms. (Please see the Kukulcan chapter; where I described, in my many dreams, my connection with creatures from the Universe, and while I am myself, my body turns into the wave-field structure.)

In that dream below, I tried to describe the crystallization process of my body as a preparation for space travel.

Dream # 41. A Gray Dumb-Bell in the Head, September 4, 1991.
I had not fallen asleep deeply yet, I still remember myself, when some substance of gray color entered my head from both sides and started to crystallize inside it. It was not a pipe, the whole thing was filled in, crystallized all at once, and it was fitting very well....

---

[7]   You will find more about our Spirit's characteristics at the end of the book in the Table of Common Characteristics.

However, when a person returns to our reality, to our world, that "plan structure around the body" shows amazing capabilities for analyzing and collecting components and for regeneration; returning these components into their previous structure, not only at the body level, but also at the level of consciousness and emotions.

Maybe while we are here on Earth, in the form of physical bodies, we are collecting some experiences into this energy field, crystal structure, named Soul or Spirit. After the biological body dies, we fly toward the Universe Consciousness with all of these new qualities that we accumulated during our life as a human in the physical, materialistic world, where the field-form from Space just cannot develop at all.[8]

Back to Amelia

When I saw her photo for the first time, it reminded me of my own mother! They looked like twin sisters! Someone told me that before we are born we choose our parents. She chose a woman who looked like her! My mother had the same as Amelia, high cheekbones, full lips, beautiful straight teeth, a small nose, and the same shape of eyelids.

---

[8] "Captured humans are often brought to play with the children of the visitors, who are described as melancholic and lethargic. The Gray children play with the blocks, which do not have letters or numbers on them--- instead, they emit different emotions when they are turned. The toys seem to indicate, that they are trying to learn how to feel. Could it be that this yearning for effect is one reason the visitors seek human contacts" (Daniel Pinchbeck, 2012 The return of Quetzalcoatl, 2006)

Julia's mother

Amelia
Julia's mother & Amelia have the same facial features

In this photo, I am near my mother. I am maybe around 2.5 or 3 years old. That day I drowned in the ocean. I remember that I was looking around me under water and I was surprised that the sun, the beach and people had suddenly disappeared and I wondered... I didn't know what to do next and how to get back. My Aunt Merry saved my life that day. Well... I drowned as Amelia and I drowned again in this lifetime, but this time at least I was lucky.

But my mother, who was the mother of the future Amelia reborn spirit, also studied medicine at the medical institute to become a doctor, worked as a doctor and attended flying school to fly small aircrafts

64

and to jump with a parachute! But it is also interesting that my father studied biology which Amelia loved.

I remember that I was *addicted* to the sky. I love Leonardo Da Vinci's paintings because of their spaces displaying the sky.

I think Amelia and I got this love for the sky from the Priest, which he studied constantly – the firmament during the day and the night sky with the stars. The same as Amelia, the Priest worked with maps. She had maps of the Earth; he had maps of the sky, the stars, and the galaxy, all full of numbers.

I remember that the sky was like a magnet for me, from an early age, calling me ... talking in my dreams ... I felt that something was there. I always wished to know what was there; I wished to touch the sky.

Once I talked about the sky with my grandmother, I was three and half years old. I asked her, "What is the sky made of?" She told me "from the air which we have around us." It was astonishing to me! I was so shocked that the same day I wished to touch the stars, and share this joy with my friends! So I called all the little children around to go with me, "I will tell you about the sky and you even can touch it," I said. Wow!

So it was a secret adventure. I organized a team of 10 to 12 kids, 4 to 6 years old. We took some little pillows and pretended that they were our backpacks. We had to cross the street where there was a deep creek, which was dry in the summer, and go down the gully. We continued going and kept on going and on talking ... and I told them what I knew about the sky.... It was a long walk because we were hoping to touch the stars, but we needed the night sky for that, right? No one saw us, because we were all small, our heads didn't go above the edge of this creek. At some point, we just sat on our pillows and stared at the night sky.

Our poor parents...! Suddenly all the small children who lived in this building had disappeared! At that time children played free around the houses and no one needed to watch them. It was a happy time.... There were no kidnappers around. As an organizer and leader of this trip, I was punished. My parents skipped the reading of my favorite fairy-tale and I had to stay home the next day....

Yes, I was *addicted* to the sky and high places. When I started traveling, the first thing I wished to see was a TV station. I arrived for the first time in Moscow at the age of 11, and the most important event was when I went to the Ostankino TV station, and sat in the restaurant and observed Moscow "from the sky above". When I was in Japan, for the first time, I ran to the TV station in Tokyo as soon as I could. I wished to see the place where I was, all at once, from sky level.

While I was a student in University, I was in Tibet, high in the mountains, studying plants, animals, and insects, for two weeks.

I woke up always early in the morning, at dawn, and climbed as high as I could. I loved to look around, far down into the valley and high onto the mountains. I loved to be very high, to see everything from a birds-eye-view.

Chasing butterflies

Once, early in the morning, I found an Alpine field where only some big, blue onion-flowers grew – round-shaped, like blue balls. They stand straight and apart – a distance of 20 cm separating them – and around 1.5 meters high. In each of them was a huge white sleeping butterfly! It looked like white triangles!

It was like the butterfly in one of my dreams but a real one this time ... so magic to see it. There were flowers all around, going far in the distance ... forever ... and on each of them there was a butterfly.... It felt as if I were in a butterfly kingdom where these little sleeping angels were all around me ... I remember I even stopped breathing....[9]

---

[9] YES, it looks like I experienced this special feeling because of the Priest.... maybe he thought he was in heaven with butterflies-souls all around him!

According to hieroglyphic texts, towards the end of the classical Maya period, there was a belief that right after death the deceased went down to the cave-homeland of his ancestors and went through a purification ritual. The souls of the buried ones came out of there in the form of butterflies that are called "the eyes of the buried ones".

When it was time to return, I collected them easily, one by one and kept eight of them between my fingers. But it was not easy to go down the mountains without the support of my hands – I had both hands up and to the side, like kids flying an imaginary airplane.... So I started to play airplane and ran down the hill. On the way down, it helped to catch the branches of some bushes for support. At one point, during this rapid descent, I almost stepped on an EFA, the most poisonous snake in the region. This snake looks like a rattle snake, with a short, piggish face and a rude attitude – it just bites – no warning, no cobra dance. BUT she is beautiful – all covered in powder-pink, innocent color! She slithered across the path and my foot stepped next to her and I felt my skin touching her but I just continued running down. It was impossible to stop anyway. From time to time you need to stop for a bit, though, or you will turn into a ball "rolling" down the hill instead of "running". I guess the Priest's knowledge taught me how to run down from the pyramid stairs without anything to support me.

When I arrived back at the camp, the students just started waking up, coming out of their tents. They were all amazed when I showed them the butterflies. We all dreamt to catch at least one like these for the collection, because this is the biggest butterfly living in Tibet! It is huge, gorgeous, and all white with two big round dots on its wings!

I let them go, all of them, at once. I took them while they were sleeping, dreaming, so it would have been easy to start spraying them with perfume and kill them for the collection. It was beautiful when all eight butterflies started flying from my hands! It was magic to see how they flew ... so big and slow ... it was unreal ... like planes....

I guess I inherited my love for adventure from Amelia, to be a tomboy like she was. *"She was a tomboy – climbing trees, sledding in the snow, and hunting"* (Richard E. Gillespie, Amelia Earhart)
http://www.tighar.org/Projects/Earhart/ResearchPape
rs/Earhart.html#2

Me the same! I love the feeling of heavy rifles in my hands. I just knew exactly what to do and how when I got my hands on an air rifle for the first time. I never killed anything in my life and will never do in future... but I love the feel of a well-made instrument of power and it is okay to use it in the shooting range.

This funny photo was taken by a celebrity French photographer; I am hunting here with a "photo-gun".

Hunting

During my life I had all kinds of animals at home. My father was the best to provide me with a variety of them.

Last year, as soon as I arrived in Kauai, Hawaii, we went with my daughter to the Kalapaki beach. It is near the Marriot hotel in Lihue and I started swimming near some big, black, lava rocks in the middle of the beach. All of a sudden, I saw this big sea turtle near me! First time in my life! I started "hunting" for the turtle. All I did was to navigate her, to swim toward the beach and the black rocks to a shallow place. When she was on top of the black rock, I lifted her up from the water by her front claws. I was able to do that when all of her body was out of the water and I could then show her to the children. A Japanese family from a cruise ship was watching me, they told me that it was "good luck" that I found a turtle. When I told them that I just arrived 20 minutes ago from Canada, and this was my first sea turtle and my first swim in Kauai, they said that I was blessed. I just loved this turtle! She came almost every day during the next 40 days to eat seaweed on those rocks. I easily recognized her by the little scratch on her back. I used to sit on the rocks for a long time, watching her swim around.

Every day, when I went swimming in the morning, in Rarotonga, on Cook Islands, the same bright tropical fish followed me! Usually, I stopped near a big, round coral and she started to swim around to try to touch my legs. I instead tried to catch her, clapping my hands together. I could continue doing this forever until I would lose interest. Yet, I continued doing it every day for three months!

Crazy fish

I flew back to Canada and returned three months later. All this time, I remember that fish and prayed that no one caught her and ate her.

I returned and she was right where I left her, following me again. Two months later, I saw some fishermen who catch all kinds of fish walking on the beach with a fish that resembled my friend. I told him my story. The fisherman smiled and told me that this particular fish tried to protect her territory! Nothing more! My illusion was gone! Now I knew that this strange fish didn't play, she actually tried to attack me a little bit to show that this was her territory!

For some reason, I just can't eat animals, for many years already, since 1985. And I never wanted to start. My friend, a monk, told me that this gives me the ability for intuition, predictions and it helps me to see what other people cannot see. The DNA which is found in animal protein has loads of information, which could disturb my metabolism and my Spirit. It also carries that fear-of-death signal which the animal produces before dying.

Many years ago, I was in China, in Beijing. I made a deal with an international publishing house and the Director was very happy.

He told me, "Today, this evening, there will be a surprise for you!"

I asked him, "What surprise? What surprise?"

However, he decided to keep it a secret. It was an invitation for dinner at the zoo restaurant, which is located in the zoo territory. There was a big round table, with many people sitting around it. The Director then lifted some of the pieces of meat from the trays, one by one, and declared, "This is meat of the eagle! This is meat of the bear! This is meat of the deer; this is meat of the snake!" and so on, and so on.

I guess there were maybe 30 or more animals on these serving plates. This was the most exotic food display I ever saw! But, I told my translator, Lu Bin, "I don't eat meat!" She asked me not to tell the director because he would go to another restaurant! Then I thought of all these people at the table, who worked in the publishing house, their dream had come true today. They would never be able to afford coming to this restaurant in their lifetime.

The salaries were very small in China at that time. But the government pays the companies for going to the restaurants during foreign guests' visits – the budget is unlimited, I guess. According to the rules, all of the company staff can go to the restaurant as well. I remember going to restaurants a few times a day with all kinds of companies and their staff.

On that day, the students and I decided to go hunting for *jerboas* in the desert. This is the cutest animal I ever saw. It is the size of a tennis ball, with a long tail and brush at the end, long ears like a rabbit, and black and white stripes! They have enormous black eyes. In the desert, the animals are mostly active at night and they need good vision. So we all climbed into the jeep and drove through the valley in the middle of the night. With the spotlights mounted on the hood of the jeep, we saw an old Muslim cemetery full of mud-houses kind of graves with moons on top instead of crosses....

Suddenly, on this dry, cracked desert soil, right in the beams of our spotlights, we saw lots of tennis balls jumping, up to a meter high. WOW!!! It was surreal ... unreal.... The trick was to jump from the moving jeep, continue running to try to catch them while they were up in the air. But the most important part of this game is to jump from the jeep and continue running as soon as you touch the ground, so you won't break a leg.... Only one of the students and I volunteered to do this ... and I loved it! It is lots of fun to catch this cute creature in your hands – this fuzzy, fluffy, lively ball. They are so naïve they never even think of biting you.... Guess what? I collected lots of them and the next day we measure their tails, ears and we weighed them. Once we completed our observations, we brought them back to the desert and let them run and jump on their home ground.

Desert Jerboa – JACULUS JACULUS

An "extraordinary" desert creature has been caught on camera for what scientists believe is the first time. Mysterious mammal caught on film By Rebecca Morelle, Science reporter, BBC News,
http://news.bbc.co.uk/2/hi/science/nature/7130484. stm

I didn't see this kind. I was dealing with the cutest, adorable ones from Central Asia, Tibet and in the website below there are good pictures to see.
http://www.terra-minora.ru/new/?page=we&type=faq4

And some others in this website:
http://www.redbook.ru/74/page40.html.
They all belong to the RED book of protected species.

The next day we were hunting for scorpions. I love this game! All you do is lift the rocks. In the desert, all living creatures hide under the rocks. So when you lift a rock, you can find anything; from scorpions to snakes, lots of insects as well, and turtles.

Amelia Reborn? Egypt

But my favorite is the pray-mantis. I was hunting for them all over the world in different countries! I just love them. Afterwards they lived in my home. They sat in a big glass container, in the same elegant position, for hours – in front of me near my computer. Occasionally, with one perfect, fast move, they caught a drosophila. I fed them honey and fruits as well.

I remember running through the jungle in the South of Japan when I heard a cicada screaming for help. I knew that something was wrong. I always pay attention when a crow is screaming, this is an indication that something special is happening in the area. I was stunned when I saw a huge green mantis hanging upside down from the branch of a tree, holding a big, fat cicada by its front legs! I grabbed the cicada, let it go and caught that elegant, gorgeous mantis instead. I already described its future life in Tokyo in the "ghost story" in the book, The Priest, by Julia SvadiHatra.

Hunting snakes in Australia
Photo by: David Holliday

76

This snake comes all the time to eat eggs and little chickens... So Julia caught her and took her far away. The owner of the place tried to do the same, but the snake always returned – this was her territory.

By the way, I found out that Malaysia has the biggest pray-mantises in the world. They're pretty big apparently, and they can make a real domestic pet.

My daughter showing the octopus I just caught!

Amelia Reborn? Egypt

It was great hunting for octopuses in the waters of the Cook Islands in the South Pacific! Some people walk on the reef in the dark with flashlights, trying to find them in the water between the rocks. People try very hard to catch them – octopuses are extremely smart. They swim very fast out of reach if you try to chase them. But I outsmarted them, I simply gave them my hand and they stuck around the hand with their long legs, and once they had a good grip, I just carried them, swimming toward the beach. And that's it!

By the way, I don't like crows. Never hunt for them. One spring I couldn't sleep because they had made a nest in a tree near my window! Every day I woke up, together with their little kids screaming for food. I was fed up and decided to fly to Japan. I woke up in my Hiro apartment the following morning at the sound of crows screaming outside the window! I just couldn't believe it. I closed my eyes and asked myself, "Am I in Canada or Japan?" I was afraid to open my eyes. When I opened them, I knew that my Canadian nightmare was pursuing me in Japan! It was 5:30 a.m. I got up and looked out the window. Near the balcony, on the cutest Japanese pine tree, there were maybe ten birds cawing their hearts out. BUT those were at least twice as big as the Canadian ones, with huge beaks! They were like eagles! I went to the kitchen, brought some potatoes and tomatoes with me to the balcony and started throwing my missiles at them. My friend, Lisa, then told me, "Don't do this because the people in the Hiro area will be the victims of those very smart and cruel crows!" Our neighbor, a professor from Europe, was also throwing potatoes at them. Later that morning, when he went out, three crows were waiting for him near the entrance and attacked him. They bit his head and face until he bled. When the new mayor ordered to rid the city of these crows, there was a huge celebration.

***

Back to the Tibet mountains

Near the place where we were camping with the students was an astonishingly beautiful waterfall. Every morning all kinds of animals came to the place to drink fresh water. I always went to the foot of the fall before sunrise, hid in the bushes and watched them. It was magic to see the light dancing through the water; it looked like a million shiny diamonds dropping down ... and all kinds of birds and animals, drinking together at the same time.

Once, I decided to climb very high, up to the top of the waterfall to see as far as I could possibly do. I was very happy and excited, so I didn't pay attention that I was way too high already, so high, in fact, that I found myself in a silly situation – I couldn't climb down to go back to camp! I just couldn't see any possibility to go down from my perch!

I remember sitting there for a long time until I suddenly saw our teacher with a group of students, very far down below. They looked like ants to me. At that moment, I decided that if I could not turn back I would jump ahead of the fall as much as I could to make sure that I would not struck any rock on the way down. It would be best for the students to find me dead right there on the little road next to the waterfall. Otherwise, many people would spend lots of time trying to find me, and most likely, they would never do. To be listed as "lost in the mountains" would be a shame and it seemed to be much better to me, at the time, to be dead and easy to find than "lost forever"! It looks like my past life's experience in Amelia's situation, when I was lost and died in the middle of the Pacific, very much affected my spirit! And my spirit was struggling and suffering from the event.

I was in a hopeless situation.... The sun was setting behind the mountains. I closed my eyes for a few minutes trying to think of what to do ... and when I opened my eyes, I saw a huge, noble deer with big antlers near me. I remember how he looked at me with his big, brown, shiny eyes. I saw his breath whiffing out of his snout – he was an impressive animal. He saw me and started running away, jumping.... It was an awesome sight. I saw him literally flying with one long jump from my left to the next rock. And then, a miracle; he showed me the way to survive and I followed in his tracks. I started to move toward the place where he landed from his first jump and found a stable ledge from which I could step and start moving down ... back to life.

Persistence – Perseverance

When I was six years old, I played with other kids outside in the street near a large drain pipe. All the kids were 8 or 9 years old and they jumped from one side to the other across a big hole in the land. In the middle of this hole there was a pipe which was going across the hole to the creek, to the other side to a wall where the cigarette factory was located.

I wished to be like these big kids. But I was too small; I couldn't jump the way they did, so I decided to climb across the pipe instead. Suddenly, boiling water started flowing through the pipe. I had already put my legs on the hot metal pipe – it was too late to go back. It was pretty high. I only wished to prove to myself that I could do it – that I could go over this pipe! I wanted to show that I was no less than these kids! So I continued to go over the pipe. When I was on the other side, the leg, which had touched the pipe, was burned. My leotard was melted into the skin on the thigh. I remember how I went to my piano lesson and played, sitting at the very edge of the chair, afraid of touching this very painful spot. Afterwards, I spent the day in school – same story – I sat at the very end of the bench and lived with this, this excruciating pain throughout the day. In the evening my parents brought me to my grandmother and left for the weekend. When she called me to take a bath…, she saw what happened. I remember that my grandfather ran to the pharmacy to buy some medicine for her heart – she had had a shock. My thigh was melted into the stocking, through the skin and up to the muscle…. Now I have a big round "kiss" imprint from that pipe on my leg – a mark of my persistence and perseverance.

Amelia Reborn? Egypt

The Priest, during my past life regression, was continuing to perform the sacrifice rituals, even when Di Cherry offered him to stop it and to change the subject.... No matter how hard it was for him personally to perform these sacrifices, he *persisted and persevered* with them, because he felt responsible....

When Amelia decided to fly around the world, she *persisted and persevered* with the idea, and she did it.

****

Now, I wish to tell you one important thing which I understood and learned for myself during the last five months, since I started studying my past lives. What people see from a distance of famous, royal people or celebrities is just a flash, a glimpse of what their life is really about. I experienced the kind of life they really have, their personal feelings from inside, and it is a hard, very stressful life, not an easy one as many people would think.

All of my past lives were full of responsibilities, intense and at the edge of most possible human capabilities. I feel uncomfortable when I hear people around me talking about meaningless things for hours. They communicate on a shallow, surface level, but with great emotions, though.... That's a waste of time. They are losing their valuable energy this way.

Each person from my past life cares about people deeply.

The queen from Atlantis had the responsibility for the well-being of her people. She was responsible for one most important part of their lives; the Energy of the Crystals. This energy supported all and each part of their activities in Atlantis.

The Priest had lots of onerous responsibilities – for the harvest, the health of his people and astrology. He was also teaching astrology; performing rituals and dealing with droughts, dry land and worrying about future harvests and his hungry people. It was overwhelming for him to sacrifice the people he knew and loved....

Amelia had the responsibility to do her best in order to prove to the world that there were new, wonderful possibilities for everyone to travel by airplanes for long distances. Secondly, she wished to prove that women can do very well, that they were no less than men (especially if some of them were men in their past lives. I can assure you that each man on the planet was a woman in his previous life, at least once.) By the way, Amelia lived at a time when most women on the planet were housewives.

I had the responsibility to invest my knowledge, abilities and skills to build a new country during perestroika, open new freedoms and new possibilities to develop the body, soul and spirit of people. During my life, I helped many talented, creative people.

I had a dream where I was an angel myself with two real pure-white wings and my guide, in my dream, told me that he and other Spirits called me DIAMOND. I ask him, "Why diamond?" He told me that when I try to help talented and creative people, I try to cut off the problems from around them which liberate them from the frictions of their every day life and make them more productive. It is interesting that kids in school also called me by that name. Kids often see things adult can't see.

I helped thousands of people change their lives on a big scale. I remember helping 1200 pearl farmers in little

Manihiki Island in the middle of the South Pacific Ocean. They told me that they had prayed and waited for help; for someone like me to come to their aid for many years. They were even ready to make me their representative in the New Zealand parliament.... Just imagine 1200 people; they didn't have a doctor or a dentist on the island... and the brokers kept them as slaves for many years by taking their pearl harvest and paying them little money for risking their lives every time they dove.

All of the people from my past lives had painful problems with children. The Atlantis woman was separated from her son for ever. The Priest sacrificed his son's life trying to save the lives of the people in his community. Amelia sacrificed her personal life and delayed the birth of her child for years.... I am glad that I fulfilled Amelia's wish and that I am a mother in this life.

Amelia died by drowning. I don't know how the life of the Atlantis Queen ended with the catastrophe they experienced, but I know that she would not have left her people and would have been with them until the end. I hope my Priest's bones were laid amid the seven graves of the other High Priests I saw in Chichen Itza.

I hope this is my last life on this planet. It looks like there is not much luck in my coming back – not too much fun or joy down here.... Or perhaps I will be re-born and just study and experience pleasure next time....

I recognize now that I am lucky in this life, because I had the rare possibility to see the chain of my past lives, the echoes from my past, and make adjustments to my future spiritual development. For example, I inherited a big "ego" from the Priest via Amelia and was finally able to shut it down in this life. As a result, I am wise now. It is like an award door opened for me that allowed me to make the connections with a Higher Power, Goddesses and Spirits, to experience the possibility to receive lessons, rare knowledge from them and improve myself.

Was Amelia MEANT TO DIE?

Today is the 28th of September. I finished writing this book in the summer. Now my editor, Roxane, has finished editing it and will complete the formatting and photo insertions today. The book will be ready to go to the publisher early next week.... BUT, I woke up this morning and remembered that I was just talking, in my dream, to my guide, my guardian Angel, about Amelia! We were in some city park, sitting on the ground and I leaned against something at my back. It was dusk.

During that dream, my guide told me that Amelia was MEANT TO DIE according to the plan! And the name for the book should be *Amelia Reborn!* This was terrible to hear after all the emotional suffering I had to endure during the hypnosis session about Amelia. These last minutes before her death make me cry each time I start reading about it again!

I asked him: "What plan? Who makes this plan?" Her death was extremely unfair!

Here is what he told me:
My life, hers and this book were planned even before we were born. The Spirit planned a few lives ahead to ensure the best outcome for the planet from the next few lives. Well..., even for me who wrote this book about it, it was a shocking thing to hear – and way too much for me to handle at once!

To plan the next few lives?

Amelia Reborn? Egypt

He told me that before the Spirit was born as Amelia, He made a plan where to be born, who to be, what to do and how to die!

The plan was...

1. To be a famous person in the era of aviation in order to have all the data of her life available for me to insert in the book, to compare her life with mine and possibly with other people's lives in this chain such as that of the Priest.

2. To disappear in this mysterious way in order to become an even more renowned person, attract attention and keep this interest alive for many years, long enough for her to be reborn and complete the goal and write the book.

3. To disappear in order to create mystery for me. To have this dream for years in my mind, ultimately to push me to go to a past life regression specialist; at first, thinking about my "little self" as a person, just wishing to achieve some level of emotional comfort while trying to get "rid of the heavy emotional burden" of a past life.

4. And afterwards find out a much bigger, serious level, and real purpose to what happened to Amelia and the reasons for her and me to be born.

Last, what my guide told me is this, "In reality, the life of just one person is not so important.... The kind of impact his or her life has on the well being of the whole planet is what is important, not only for the people, but also for nature, plants and animals."

I woke up then and started thinking about it...

And I remembered this sentence:
Ironically Amelia Earhart has become more famous for disappearing than for her many real aviation achievements.
http://www.acepilots.com/earhart.html

Yes, if Amelia did not die in this mysterious fashion, perhaps she would have been one among many other popular, pioneering aviators and live a long and happy life. However, it was her final flight that made her life a legacy.

I would not have had repeating dreams for years about a woman disappearing before the Second World War started. My guardian angel would never have shown me, in my dream, this "documentary movie about this woman-pilot's life" and I would never have remembered that, in the dream, I recognized the aircraft, how to operate it and screamed, "This is me!" or afterwards ask myself, "What happened with me then?"

I would never have gone and asked a hypnosis specialist, Diana Cherry, for help to understand what this was all about? If I would have only one past life as a Priest, it would have been a *nice* book, but fewer people would have paid attention to it, found it and read it!

Lots of spiritual books are available. But putting Amelia's life in front of millions of people interested in what happened to her will attract their attention to this book and they will read it.

It will be a key word, like a password, for people to open the door to find, to study and to acquire serious fundamental knowledge about their own chain of lives and to start thinking about their own Spirit development. It will be useful, important and priceless for each and everyone in the world to know.

What is the nature of YOUR Soul or Spirit? What happens to YOUR SOUL after death? When this life is finished, will it be the end of everything? Or is it only one little step among many that a person has taken already – walking through the chain of lives, still having many to walk in the future?

The devil, Lucifer, the prince of destruction, of darkness and ugliness is not the one who created people. God created people to be *Creative*, pure of heart and thoughts and to try to do the best they can to make this world, happier, brighter, cleaner and more beautiful by their mere presence (EXISTENCE).

There will be a time when each and every one of us will die and will go to the Spirit world and reap the "harvest" of this life which has just passed. What did he gain? Maybe lots of new knowledge, new abilities, skills, appreciation from the people around him for the gift of love and happiness he imparted to them? It will be an astonishingly sad moment for someone who will deeply regret that he did something wrong during his life for his family and the people around him. Or maybe with his power and intellect, he initiated the huge destruction of a society, country, or nature on the planet!

Maybe someone tried to make money and acquired fame and fortune – an "image" – during his life, while destroying forests or oceans, or a whole country, and killing many people. However, then, he will be sitting in line waiting for his judgment with empty hands, because he just couldn't bring with him money or anything from his life to that place. Perhaps he will feel that he was sadly misinformed! The devil simply tricked him, attracted him to money and material possessions which became a "big thing" during his life. He spent all of his energy working on it very hard, but the real "gold" is now in someone else's hands – in the hands of those who were creative and improved their positive quality... how unfair, he will say!

"What goes round comes round...."

Now I understand the enormous responsibility that has been bestowed upon me to try to bring this book to the people. And I cry for Amelia who lost her life so young in order to help millions of people understand and prove that our Spirit does not die after death and to demonstrate it through her own example.

My guide told me that I should study Amelia's life and that I will find much more common between the two of us than I first observed! But I am running out of time now; I need to rush, even to add this part ... is going to be difficult! YES, I feel guilty! Amelia's entire life was a "preparation" for my book and I studied only one website about her!

Well, to be honest, I did not pay special attention to Amelia's chapter. She was just one from a few other people from my past lives, so I checked only one website. I should have spent more time and studied more about her, and compared more characteristics, but the book is ready and I have no time to do this now....

By the way, when I said, "I leaned against something at my back" at the beginning of my dream, the "something" was Amelia's bronze statue! I didn't even know that such a statue existed.

While I was writing an email to Roxane, I checked Amelia's website to find out what this statue looks like,

and I ended up in her museum, the house where she was born. I clicked FUN Facts about Amelia.
http://www.ameliaearhartmuseum.org/AmeliaEarhart/AEFunFacts.htm

Well.., my guide was right as usual:

- Amelia had a younger sister, me too!
- Amelia had a *black dog* and I had a black dog; his name was Black Ball. He had the same nature as Amelia's dog had; he was very protective, angry and ferocious!
- Amelia had the middle name *Mary*. My aunt's name is Merry. She is living in Russia and bears an English name – because her father read an English book once and he liked the name. My aunt told me that there was a problem with her birth certificate 65 years ago in Russia – an English name for a Russian girl was not acceptable in those days. But he wanted it no matter what and got it for her!
- Amelia had lots of imaginary friends, playmates, horses.... Well..., that's only because she saw them, in the same way I see them. There were always Spirits around her as there are around me.
- One of her playmates was named *Laura* – in school, my girlfriend's name was Laura!
- *Amelia named the twin maple trees in her grandparent's Atchison front yard Philemon and Baucus after a husband and wife in Greek mythology.* This was astonishing to me! I named two huge trees here in English Bay which grow from the same roots with my husband's and my name. One tree blossomed with white flowers – mine, the second one never had flowers but had a luxuriant crown of leaves. When my husband needed to move definitively to Europe, years ago, his tree suddenly died, and soon afterwards, it was cut down by the city's garden maintenance department!

- And one last funny one!
Can you imagine the same black creatures following Amelia and me in her and my life?
"During her childhood, Amelia invented a tribe of imaginary small black creatures she called Dee-Jays. Described as a cross between a Krazy Kat cartoon and a jabberwocky, the creatures were often blamed for Amelia's own irresponsible behavior, such as: talking out of turn, eating the last piece of candy, or when something turned up lost."
Now, do you remember how Dream # 5 starts – The Upper Kingdom, October 24, 1993?
"It was some terrible, black, big and hairy creature."
And in Dream # 27 – Hundreds of Followers – Rubies, November 8, 2003; do you remember the wet hairy creature at the end of the dream?
"One scene was repeated several times. I opened the door from the room to the street. And some wild creatures, like wet, little dogs wanted to rush into the place where we were sitting."
Dream # 38 – A Man of the Forest – His Name, December 13, 1991
But it was not from our life. This reminds me of something like Jabberwocky in Lewis Carroll. I understood, they understood. But here I cannot understand at all. In Jabberwocky there is a substantive and adjective. But here there were neither of them. It was an event from my other life.

Can you believe it? I even tell in my dream that this was an event from my other life. This dream was in 1991, when I didn't have any idea that we have many lives and this at a time when I was living another life, when I was living as Amelia, her life!

I guess that's enough comparisons for one day....

91

Amelia Reborn? Egypt

Amelia wrote: *"My ambition is to have this wonderful gift produce practical result for the future of commercial flying and for the women who may want to fly tomorrow's planes."*

My ambition in this life is that this book will be a gift for everyone living on the planet, to pass on the rare knowledge that the Spirit of the people has ETERNAL LIFE and does not die after the body dies. And I proved this with Amelia and the Maya Priest's help. Spirit just continues its own development in the next newborn baby body. All skills, knowledge and habits people accumulated during their lifetime are transferred through the chain of their lives. This is a valuable, priceless property of the Spirit. It will never lose value.

It is important to know; especially now, with the melt down of the economy, the whole world is scared and everything is losing value. It seems that there is no stable ground to stand on.

The most important thing is that you got the idea why *Amelia was meant to die...* and now I can say it easily, without stopping to take a breath, as I did when I heard it for the first time from my guide in my dream today.

After this dream, I can add one more version to the collection of Disappearance Speculations of Amelia Earhart. It may sound really strange, but as for me after the crazy things which happened during the production of this book, I think it is possible. Remember the unexplained force which lifted a man from his chair, sent him to his locker room, and pushed him to bring his laptop to my door hours before my laptop burned out so that I could continue writing this book on his computer? And many other cases.... It looks like a "team" of Spirits is involved and supports me in writing this book.

I remember the story of the "Miracle man" who lives in Brazil. He incorporated 33 Spirits entities into his body. There were doctors among them, and he, in a split second, performed invisible surgeries through these entities and treated up to 600 people a day! (*The Miracle Man: The Life Story of João de Deus, by Robert Pellegrino-Ostrich. Extracted from his book Published in 1997, ©1997/1998. All rights reserved.*) [1]

If it was the Spirit's goal to make Amelia disappear mysteriously, in order to give people knowledge that the Spirit is eternal and never dies, it is very important to live a creative spiritual life. The Spirit manages to do this perfectly: *"The mysterious fate of the larger than life woman flyer tugged at the public's consciousness. No trace of the craft was ever found – although an extensive coordinated search was carried out by the Navy and Coast Guard. Despite the efforts of 66 aircraft and 9 ships and an expenditure of an estimated 4 million dollars, authorized by President Franklin D. Roosevelt, their fate remained a mystery."*

PS:
Dear Readers,
When you read "Amelia Reborn" or "The Re-birth of an Atlantean Queen", you will probably notice that Julia talks about "proofs". In one instance, she says that finding someone's bones is further "proof" they are Amelia's bones. This is to be taken in context. This assertion stems from her extensive experience with the Spirits.
It was very strange, in fact. I modified the above sentence twice, and twice inexplicably the words "...they were Amelia's bones" came out in the final copy. I could not believe my eyes. I was up in arms. The final copies of these two books were already at the printer. This was beyond anything I had ever experienced before. I was going nuts. I phoned Julia. She simply told me, "Please bear in mind; Spirits can move in the strangest and most unexpected way."
Roxane Christ
Author/Editor

Chapter 2

Egypt

During my life I had many dreams about Egypt, below are two of them. This person, an ancient EGYPTIAN PRIEST or Pharaoh, contacted me from time to time in my dreams for the last 18 years....

Dream # 2
The Blue Vessel of an Egyptian Priest & Pharaoh, January 10, 1992

There is a large, blue vessel, high above me, like a mirror, but situated a bit higher – since I cannot see my reflection in it. And from it – there is a way out to the other side of the Earth ... or another planet, a galaxy. There is the face of a person, looking at me from that side....

Who is on that side?
He looks straight ahead, but it is not a face he has; it is some kind of mask,[10] like melted wax has been poured over his features. Maybe this is why he does not speak – he is afraid to break the mask. Or maybe he never talks. The mask is like that of a Pharaoh; he does not seem to be alive. On this mask there are painted eyes; they are contoured. But the head is so strange.... It is not fluorescent, but translucent – blue inside and dull outside. His arms (hands?) are also painted – pasted with the white coating. And the rest of the body and

---

[10] The eyes are painted and contoured around bright lapis-lazuli, under the white coating of the face – they are transparent. This impression of him; it may be horrifying to the common people.

hair are covered with clothes. People think that he's like that all over and that his blood is blue.[11]

I see him not for the first time, I knew him, and he knows me. I also see a green emerald. I thought it is a vessel – but the emerald is inside it. In the vessel there is a ray – coming from the crystal. There, where you look – there is a crystal. This person can turn into a crystal. Or his sheath is of green color. The ray is not sharp; it is soft, pleasant. The name is Ashur, no, I cannot pronounce it. Ashar ... maybe ... He is a friend. He is an astrologist. His name and his essence are connected with the green emerald color, and with a star. It is the color of the sea – a light greenish shade. The star defines his aim, purposes, etc. He knows the stars very well. Now I see the Yellow planet with his eyes, and on the side of it, there is a red line. I also see a Red Planet. It is over the horizon. It is in his time. In a sense – his star is like Uranus, but because of its softness in appearance, I feel it's like Neptune. The light is soft, not sharp.

He is very clever, and he is the main figure there. His main purpose – not the problems with the Pharaoh, or the construction – is to pass his knowledge onto his successor. It is the most important thing for him, he is thinking about it all the time. Everything should be reflected, like in a mirror; everything should be polished. The rest is trifle. Only one per cent of his knowledge is used in life. That is why all of the problems of the Empire are all mere trifles. It is like a gem which is passed from one generation onto the next. In this state, the most important thing is not a Pharaoh,

---

[11] Maybe this is the way how pharaohs colored their faces to look like their Atlanteans teachers, Sumerians or even people from the future?

but this knowledge. This is the most valuable thing in the Empire.

His knowledge comes from strange people. They are wearing white, silvery clothes. Like that snake in the Turkmenistan Desert – as if made of aluminum. They are dressed in some sort of spacesuit of a square shape, like truncated pyramids. There are squares on their heads. And around the neck there are some lines, similar to those of the pharaohs. They look like pharaohs. But they are similar to a dragon-fly shedding its skin. And in the beginning it was made as if from ... some kind of wax ... layers of translucent synthetics. People painted it from some substances and the pharaohs copied it. Those, who were giving them knowledge – on the sides of their heads, where the ears are, their clothes were pleated like an accordion. The Pharaohs started copying them and painted such long eyes on their drawings because of that. These people gave this knowledge, and afterwards it was passed on during the life of a man. Besides the main Priest, there were some others, less significant. Each of them had just one part ... but everything he was giving, he gave only to one person. He is like a queen bee; everybody valued the knowledge he passed on. But if something had happened to him, the others probably could restore it part by part.

This knowledge is like a sphere which is painted over with parallel lines. These are levels of immersion. As soon as it moves from one level to another, the saturation of information (energy) takes place. If he wants to know, then he knows right away what level is needed. It is similar to a rainbow. The most important thing is the transition between the levels, the ability to get into the right color. It is important to know the task and to have a purpose. For those who can do it, it is very simple. When someone knows the question, one just goes through the levels, and the right field is reacting to it. It is like a fog, a very thick fog, the person submerges into it. Different planets are masters over these colors. The color comes from these planets. For example, when he thinks about a Red planet – he thinks about war, etc.

How does he work...?

His head is of a strange shape – a long skull. The head is bald; probably under it, all of it is artificial. It is long and flat, squeezed on both sides. And in the place where the fontanel is, there is something that was inserted – some sort of lens. When he was a baby – something round was inserted in his skull – it was stuck between the bones. *Then they pressed it. The skull was growing, and the bones in the fontanel did not knit.* If the lens was to be made a little bigger, the person could have died. The ray *(from the crystal)* would get in and the brain would not be able to endure the pressure. However, the bigger the lens, the more the power the person had. The width of the lens was very important. This thing is right at the crossing with the third eye. With the lens it can be done four times a year, at the change of seasons. It is better when there are two dates – the Equinox – on the equinoxes, they do some corrections.

There is a strange animal beside him. It has stripes all over its body, and the face is narrow, like that of a dog. It is about the size of a medium-sized dog, bigger than a cat. Its ears are sticking up like those of a fox. It has almost no fur. It senses everything. On its neck, there is a golden hoop and stripes and two or three stripes on its back. Those pharaohs were from some other planets, maybe, and they drew these stripes on their heads to imitate those of an animal.

These animals could talk to the Priests. They could prompt the solutions. They put a similar crystal on their heads. (How terrible!) Between their ears, there was something the shape of an olive – like an eye looking from a crystal, a lens. Maybe they used it for meditation.

He may have felt that this little creature (animal) knew where the truth was, and could correct it. It perceived the intentions, color, planets, and influences. There were eight or nine senses besides the common ones. Here there were two of them – him and the animal. They had a question. They had some sort of *aquarium*, where the liquids merged together (90% of it). Now they were merging, but they did not merge as such. A man (a human being) had a set of senses to feel things. This animal also had it. When there were intentions – the feelings came alive. And the animal felt the range of it, fed it, rectified it, and helped identify the positions, like on a map. The animals didn't have words, nor logic, no abstract mind, the things humans invented in their world and ultimately blocked out. That is why the animals can feel and sense things better than humans do. It perceives a man and helps him. The main thing for the animal is those ten senses from the *aquarium*. The animal senses a human, and the human being does not need to feel an animal. For the animal, the person is like a father, mother and for his part, the animal is a tamed one. They don't look like cats; the face is not flat, but long.[12]

---

[12] Here is what the Priest-pharaoh, his animal and Maya have in common: Arguelles was exploring the Maya conception of time, energy and consciousness. The Mayas actually possessed a more advance science than we do: What distinguishes Mayan science from present day science is it is a system operating within a galactic frame." With this synthesizing and holistic worldview, based on mind as the foundation of the universe, inseparable from time and space, "not only do the Mayas challenge our science, but they play with our myths". The basic goal of Mayan civilization, underlying their obsession with astronomical orbits and vast cycles of time, was synchronicity,

Who is he connected with?

The Priest is connected with me. This connection is very important for him. Maybe in the future, through generations, I must become his student, and the generations were interrupted. He knew that the following should have been this creature, but he saw later, that between them there is a generation gap. And he transcends his knowledge through his mind to him, and the other one absorbs it in his dream, but he does not realize it. But maybe he sees a chain of people. He values the diapason of life, the chain of people, from one to another via this tube, going through centuries. They could find with their minds the time period of humanity. And to define those who will be born in the future, they put together these people in one line and transfer them through the tube. This is their duty, obligation – this channel is supposed to be eternal. At any moment there could be a necessity for this channel to ring a bell, and then the person will come out. *Nobody knew that there was this sprout in the earth – but it is growing.*[13] It is right. And it is an axiom.

---

synchro-astronization, or what Arguelles calls "harmonic resonance". Their "exquisitely proportioned" numbers' system was not primarily a counting code, but "a means for recording harmonic calibrations that relate not just to space-time positioning, but to resonant qualities of being and experience.
Maya intentionally left behind a trove of secret knowledge, hidden teaching on the nature of time and being. This information was not just some quantity of statistic or facts, but a new pattern that had to be sensed and felt as well as logically grasped. To receive a new pattern, one must be open to it. The essence of information...is not its content but its resonance", he wrote, "This is why feeling or sensing things is so important. To sense the resonance of incoming information co-create a resonant field".
[13] I just found out that it is the symbol of reincarnation, or new life, in Maya.

Does he have enemies?

The Priest did not have enemies – only in time, only in the future. There could be others who would want to acquire this knowledge – but without initiation. They were imposing themselves from the outside. It is unnatural – they are enemies.

If he chooses a successor – the one could be any person, but he sees and knows whether the one is capable to be that successor. But from the early babyhood – even before birth – they predict when the time of conception should take place and they know then when the infant will be born. It is very important – when the sun goes down, in the first month after the birth – it is important to insert the lens. The lens is replaced by another when the child is 5 or 6 years old. After that, once again, it is replaced at the age of 12 or 13, and for the last time, at the age of 19 or 20.

What does Lucifer think of it?

He is the one who is deadly scared of it. He wants all this but he knows that he, himself, could burn to death. He does not envisage the depth and enormity of all this; he does not have enough energy to understand it all. He only suspects all this; the knowledge, abilities, and capacities. But he does not know the reasons and roots, and does not even know what we were just talking about. He knows that there is a very strong, white knowledge. It is very easy for him, like champagne bubbles; he does not have time to capture them, to feel them. He has the physique – the body, the mind – but they are all different. It is like a metal that could not understand (or become) a soap bubble.

He turns from black into white when he flares up. His anger is the only expression of his creativity, the only possible one. He is like a metal, which is white hot. But there are limits to his capabilities, he cannot transform himself, he loses energy. He knows that, and he is afraid of this condition. He can kill, cold-bloodedly, ruthlessly. He cannot be controlled in such a state. Otherwise his machination would be over. He could melt, disappear. He could transcend into the light substance. Lucifer. He is dark, but he also can produce light. Creative energy destroys him.

Where do the enemies come from?
He is not an enemy of the Priest. He can be the weapon of the enemies, who appeared in time, who weren't there before. He is a blindfolded weapon. He is a terminator. The Priest did not have him then. He appeared later. All the enemies appeared and stopped the normal development on the Earth in 2341. (Perhaps this figure is from the Mayan Calendar...?)

The destruction came much later – normal people with normal brains became sick. It was like an infection, a virus. They stopped everybody, turned them back. *People lost their connection with the parallel worlds, lost the integrity of development. Before, they were walking in step, in one stream with their teachers. But they stopped, dropped back, lost the sense of knowledge.* These evil people now want just one thing – to destroy everyone good in their dreams.

I see a lizard with blue skin; it is shining with all colors. I feel unusual scent of flowers.... It started on Thursday, when there was a wind. I see now, how my guide, with strong shoulder is sitting on that sphere, where a big woman was standing before.... He sends the lizard to me. It brought me two little beads in its mouth, both transparent. The first one is white, like a crystal; the other is black like obsidian.

And the eye of the lizard is half black half white ... the transparent, light-blue wings of a dragon-fly, are very

beautiful. There are not of a dragon-fly itself, they are just these pallets... (Paulo Coelho) [2]
http://www.paulocoelho.com.br/russ/index.html

****

Many people, over time, have made a connection between the form of the skull and intellectual and social superiority. For example, the Chinese "wise man" had to have a head in the shape of a cone.

There is information about the ritual of drilling the skull in Tibetan tradition – in order to "open the third eye". Currently, in Africa they pierce numerous little holes all over the skull surface, even producing blood. The initial purpose of such an operation is to make an opening in the skull bone.

In the spring of 1943, the US military started building landing strips for their aircrafts on the small island of Schemia, located in the Pacific Ocean. Twelve feet beneath the surface, they found a cemetery of giants. They found the bones of giant people – six to eight meters tall – together with the bones of mammoths and giant rhinoceroses. They were all found in the sand stratum which was at ground level during their existence. All human skulls which, by the way, were 60 cm. long, had a high, straight forehead – the same features and shape as people have right now. The most interesting find for me was that each skull had a hole 2 inches wide in it which looked like it had been covered only with skin. No one knows how or why this hole was made, or what sort of ritual the person underwent before its death to get this hole in its skull. Some think that maybe it helped their Spirits to escape freely after death. I guess, these people were "relatives" or in the same "business" as my friends, the Pharaoh – the Priest, who had the same kind of hole in their skulls, and who made another one in their animals' heads, using this process during their lives successfully. The Editor of "Fate" magazine has contact information for three witnesses who were on Schemia Island at the time of the excavation.

The Aravacs had their heads flattened out. This observation made by Spanish conquistadors was proved by a study of ancient skulls recently exhumed in Guadeloupe. In Peru, skulls in the shape of cones were found in the tombs of Paraks. Some people in America managed to open the cranial seams of newborn babies with a piece of wood in order to direct the brain substance upwards. Depending on the caste, the occipital (the bone at the back of the scull) of a person was made either flat or elongated. The head of the heir of the throne of the Great Incas was deformed in order to make his features more regular and symmetrical.

(Religious therapeutic rituals and their role in shaping sotsiotipa; Andrew G. Safronov,
safronov@3s.kharkov.ua)

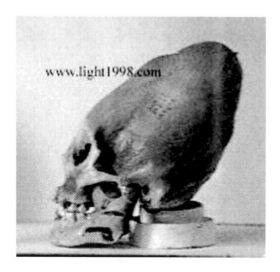

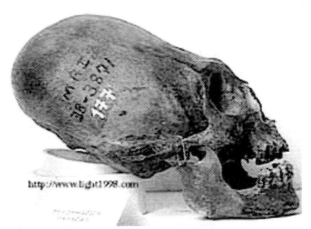

Long human skulls

(*Coneheads.* Researcher Robert Connolly photographed this strange elongated skull in 1995. It was found in South America and is estimated to be tens of thousands of years old. http://www.light1998.com/Weird-Skeletons/Weird-Skeletons.htm). [7]

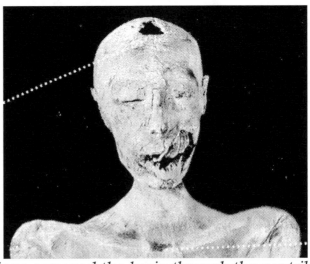

Egyptians removed the brain through the nostrils. Why there is a hole on the top of the head, no one knows. (Discovery Magazine, April 2009)

The associate producer of the CD ROM of the movie called "The Secrets of Stargate", Joel Mills, had learned that I had in my possession photographs that could prove that the movie "Stargate" was based on historical fact. Mills felt these giant skulls were proof that the ancient pharaohs the same elongated skulls hidden under their crown head-dress. I pointed out to him that Egypt's King Akhenaton and his daughters were proud of their distinct features (elongated skulls) and the true facts of this royal family are shrouded in controversy. Some historians point out that the giant skulls of this family are a deformity caused by inbreeding. Others discount this and claim that it is the art style of the Armana period. The secret society, known as the Rosicrucian, place King Akhenaton on their highest pedestal by reconstructing his statue and main temple at their head office in San Jose, California. Mills felt the world needed to see the photographs to understand that ancient skulls of extraordinary dimensions could be found at other major archaeological sites around the world, in particular, the Nasca Line and the ruins of Peru.... in the shadows of the Cheops pyramids in Egypt... and the ancient Mayan ruins of Central America... The Triangle of the Ancient Gods. In Mexico we found the same types of skulls in a museum in Merida, a city close to the ruins of Palenque. Lord Shield Pascal had the same elongated skull, an image which is found engraved on his tomb. Erich Von Daniken has described the drawings as Pascal sitting in a rocket ship. Meanwhile in Egypt, King Akhenaton was also regarded as a heretic and all information about this king was obliterated until just recently. These findings prove that the rulers of these advanced societies all shared the common bond of huge skulls and brains that probably provided them with superior intelligence. This information has been shared by secret societies and religious leaders for hundreds of years and up until now they had decided

to keep these secrets for themselves. All who first see the pictures feel... "They show proof of beings from another world."[14] It seems that these conclusions were deemed to be too shocking for the average person and that these skulls were to be dismissed as deformities and hidden far from public view.
Joe Mills –

(http://www.light1998.com/ALIEN-SKULLS/ALIEN-SKULLS.htm) [8]

Connected with my friends from my dreams, the Priest and Pharaoh, or not? But the Sumerian civilization was located not far away from Egypt. Ashur was a Sumerian God. I try to pronounce it, in my dream, as *Ashar* as well.

Ashur is the main god of Assyria (sky god) (Assyrian) – at Assur. Below Ashur there is also Inanna, or Inanna, the goddess of love and war (Sumerian) – in the E'anna temple – Uruk.

In Mesopotamian mythology, according to Wikipedia, the free encyclopedia, Ishtar (a.k.a. Sumerian "Inanna"), the Queen of the Heavens and goddess of love and war, was associated with Venus.
(http://en.wikipedia.org/wiki/Sumerian_mythology)
Anshar – http://www.crystalinks.com/sumergods.html

---

[14] All of these people with long skulls are relatives of the descendants of either the Nephilim or Neferu civilizations, who lived on the Earth a long time ago and had common children with the people from Earth, who were named as gods, goddesses or kings in different cultures – more about it in the Violet Field chapter.

Travel to Egypt, May 2008

During my life – in the last 18 years at least – I had many dreams about this person from ancient Egypt. Sometimes he was my guide, teacher in my dreams for a few months. After that, there was no contact for a time, and then, after a few months or even years, he would appear again. To make the story complete, I decided to visit Egypt. I was advised by Roxane, my editor, to make the trip, and I am glad I took her advice. Some amazing things happened to me while I was there and these events solved the mystery which I carried for years. This trip made it clear what this was all about. I am planning to do a reading with Di Cherry as well to reconnect with *him* and find out more about him and me, and my ties with Egypt.

Wall of the Cheops pyramid

Amelia Reborn? Egypt

I was Julia's private tour guide and driver in Giza, Egypt. The first morning we arrived at the pyramid's site, I started to tell her about the history of the Cheops pyramid.

During my talk I asked her if she felt something from the pyramid, maybe some special energy or something like this. Instead of answering, she pointed to her legs and to my surprise; I saw big goose bumps covering all of her legs! It continued with her getting these goose bumps from time to time during my talk. Obviously, she did feel something really strong!

At the moment, when I started to mention to her that the mummies were removed from the pyramids and were now in a museum, she changed dramatically. Suddenly, without any explanation, she started to be extremely angry about it! I was very surprised.... She started talking very emotionally, with gesticulations and loudly.... It felt like her own body was removed!

I am glad that there is a big space around the pyramids and we were far away from the other tourists, because suddenly from a very polite, dignified, courteous, quiet, Canadian girl, she changed into some angry, real ancient person! Julia just changed completely! I never experienced something like this in my life before. It was obvious that she tried to stop herself to behave in a normal way, but she just couldn't!

I felt that it was much easier for her to go with this strange "flow" than to keep it inside....This energy or I don't know even how to name it – it was coming from her independently from her own will. And it surprised her not less than me. At some point I was even scared....

Julia asked me to bring her to the real pharaoh's palace where they lived during their lives. She had a strong urge to visit their real ancient home or at least the place where it was before, where they lived. Not this "graveyard" with pyramids where people were only buried and that were empty for thousands of years. Yes, normal ordinary people were not allowed to visit this place and for thousands of years these pyramids were in great silence. But the problem was that no one knew where the pharaohs or ancient people lived! It is somewhere deep under the sand and I couldn't help her with this. Julia felt – had in her mind – some real ancient house, and she was ready to drive around with me, hoping to find it! She said that she started have a deep feeling that she missed it very much and she understood that it sounded really strange, but something like this already happened to her a few months ago in Mexico near another pyramid and she found that it was the place where she lived before in Mexico. Now it was repeating itself with the Giza pyramid's place. She had a clear experience of déjà-vu and felt that she lived here a long time ago.

YES, there was a very strange feeling about her. I was her personal guide during 4 days and this feeling never left me. It felt like two people lived inside her and she switched from one to the other without warning. As soon as we talked about ancient subjects or we were near the pyramids, she instantly turned to that other ancient side of hers...her voice, face and the way she talked and acted changed instantly at the same time!

I can tell you: I meet all kinds of tourists every day – for many years, but she is the only one who was like this. It was not even a feeling. Anyone who was near us saw it, this change, with their own eyes. From my point of view and maybe it sounds unusual, in some way she belongs to this ancient people or this family or was in touch with these ancient rituals and she knew the way it should be performed immediately. And when the rules were broken it upset her deeply. Those first hours when I witnessed *this unusual behavior of hers, I decided to bring her to my spiritual teacher, Samir, who is working at the "Atlantis" oils, healing and well-being centre. His place is near the pyramid site. It was the right decision. He explained to her and me what this was all about.*

Mohamed Abas Fattah, tour guide, Egypt, Cairo

Mohamed Abas (my guide) and Mr. Samir

Yes, Mohamed had his opinion. I suddenly completely changed near the pyramid. It was interesting that I never paid attention to Egypt history during my life.... *(The following paragraphs will show you the extent of my ignorance in this regard.)*

Yes, I was extremely upset that the mummies were removed from the pyramids and sarcophaguses. Since the trip, this feeling is still there; it never left me. I continue to feel guilty and ashamed for the people who did this.

On my last day in Egypt, on the way to the airport, I visited the Cairo museum. I bought a ticket to see the golden Tutankhamen mask and other golden treasures, but instead, by mistake, I ended up in the mummies' room! When I saw them, I changed instantly again! Lucky I was totally alone there. The problem was that *I wanted* and I began talking to the mummies with my full voice..., *with a totally clear mind.* I repeated to them again and again, "I am very sorry, I am very sorry, I am very sorry. I feel very sorry for the people who did this serious mistake and took you from your sarcophaguses and pyramids." There were 13 mummies there, mostly Egyptian kings and princesses, all gathered in one room, laid on tables, like in a morgue, side by side.

I stayed near the wise, the greatest – King Ramses II. He ruled Egypt for 65 years! And now, without the simple respect due to the common man, his body has been laid down in this glass box like an exhibit – without a coffin even! And everyone going near him looks and points at him! How humiliating!

He ended up without his own place in the cemetery! How unfair! Any ordinary human being has a place of final rest. I am sure his spirit is extremely angry! I felt this huge spirit-tension atmosphere in that room. I could almost hear how they all started screaming and complaining to me!

YES, it was a big, shameful mistake on the part of that archeologist and for the government of Egypt to follow the archeologist's decision! As for me, it is okay that they took all this gold and treasures for themselves or brought them to the museum. I agree, "Just take it!" Even though I know all of these special tools, these precious objects, played a very important part in the rituals during and after the burial of the mummies. I am still okay that these treasures ended up in the museum. BUT why pulling the mummies out of their sarcophaguses and pyramids? [15]Why did you put them in these damn glass boxes? WHY?

Someone simply tried to make some extra money by taking US$18 from the tourists to show the mummies of the great Egyptian kings to everyone – when they already took their priceless, golden treasures and made a fortune from these artifacts. It was still not enough. What a bunch of greedy people they were! Where was their pride of their great history and culture? There should not be any acceptable apology or forgiveness for this! These people deserve punishment and they got it! I am still angry about it and it looks like it will never change unless the mummies are placed back where they were meant to be.

In modern law terms I can say, "Their tombs were private property and no one's business or right to enter their mausoleums and do what they did." I am almost ready to sue all of them, to drag them through the courts on behalf of the ancient people in order to protect their privacy. These kings do not have any relatives who could protect and support them....

It is interesting that I am a Libra, the most peaceful sign of all zodiac signs. The Libra sign is very calm, quiet and private, until someone disturb his or her privacy. If

---

[15] Pyramids were built according to the plan brought to the Earth by Neferu for easy connection with them. Dead pharaohs, in many cases, were Priests who, with great purposes, were placed in to the pyramids for connecting their Spirits with Neferu and help the rest of the living Egyptian people with their needs. It is the same as the person, who was sacrificed as a "messenger" to the God in *The Priest* chapter.

a Libra starts a fight, it will be only for one important reason: to restore peace.

Two of the mummies had flowers around their bodies and I felt that I knew these flowers. I know their fragrance; I even started seeing those ancient times, the blue sky, the white limestone around us, and how these flowers grew in the desert.... For some reason, I felt myself very close to these people, who now lay as mummies in these glass boxes. I felt that I knew some of them personally. I was grieving and felt deep sorrow for them....

When I packed in Canada to go to Europe and I knew that there was a possibility for me to visit Egypt, I put my golden outfit – golden pants, top and jacket – with gold jewelry in my bags. I also added some deep blue pieces. I knew these clothes were going to be in great harmony with Egypt. So, I wanted to wear my golden outfit when I went to the Egyptian museum. I felt it was the outfit I needed to wear in this instance. But the tour guide stopped me and said that it would attract a lot of attention in the museum, because I am an attractive European girl, a model with very long golden hair... and we already had problems with the local people following us in Giza all the time.

I didn't care if I drew attention on me. But my tour guide persisted and advised me not to go to the museum in this outfit because it would be a problem for him to try to keep me safe. (I was never afraid of people. I talked to anyone at any level – from presidents to homeless people in the street. People from villages are my favorite kind; they are closest to nature and very spiritual.) Anyway, he told me that he would not drive me to the museum if I wore the golden outfit. That day was a unique opportunity for me to visit the museum and maybe seeing the mummies. I thought there would only be one or two.... So I ended up wearing my best dress for meeting kings and queens and to pay them my respects.

Yes, he was right; my presence in that museum drew a lot of attention. Everyone who worked there waved to me and tried talking to me until, finally, all of them followed me to the exit and outside on the street. They even took me everywhere – free of charge – to another room where the Tutankhamen treasures were displayed. By the way, I didn't wear anything short or sexy; I was in my favorite, long, silk dress from Saint Barth Island in the Caribbean.

Last year, after I visited the unique exhibition of "Body World" by the talented Dr. Gunther von Hagens, I even thought of donating my body for "plastination" in order to preserve it, (www.bodyworlds.com). [9] But the fact that I would be another exhibit in a glass box for the viewing of crowds of people like King Ramses II stopped me from carrying out with this idea. For some reason, I was attracted to this king more than to the others. I saw a few dreams about him during my life.

A few years ago, I visited a Russian monastery which is in the middle of Moscow. In a beautiful silver coffin, with lots of fresh flowers around it, there were the remains of a holy woman named Matrona. I was envious. I wished I could be lying there instead of her.... For some reason, I feel that it is very important to preserve the body after death. I suspect I know now why I cared about all this..., after I visited Egypt and I knew that I was a Priest in Chichen Itza in my past life.

My tour guide, Mohamed Abas, brought me to see the Light and Sound Show.

It was interesting that when I was in the plane on the way to Egypt, I started thinking about the pyramids. In my vision, I saw a round shape with turquoise, blue color, and near it, there was another round shape with pink and green colors. Very unusual colors. I didn't have any idea what these colors meant until I was near the pyramids the next morning. They were lights placed in a row, facing the pyramids, which were used for this Light and Sound Show.

Round shaped lights – turquoise-blue, violet-pink, and yellow.

It was a spectacular show with great sound and superb laser effects. It was an enchanting display of music and colors on the Pyramids and Sphinx. Everyone enjoyed it very much! It was a little bit cold with the wind blowing through the night in the desert. But they had warm blankets available for everyone.

During that show it was said how great and special each of the three pharaohs was and in which pyramid they were located. Also, they said that we should respect the enormous effort on the part of 100,000 people who worked very hard to build the great pyramids. It was mentioned that a special rock covered the entrance of the pyramid to hide the real entranceway to the place where the sarcophagus was located. It was made in order to confuse the intruders when they would try to go in.

Yet, after all this, amazingly enough, it seemed absolutely normal to everyone who saw the show and the people of Egypt that the bodies of those pharaohs were ultimately removed from the pyramids! Impossible!

Can you imagine yourself in the pharaoh's situation, when for many years you had your pyramid planned and built with great purpose and huge effort by devoted people, it is broken into, and without any respect for the sanctity of your final resting place, your dead body is pulled out and put in a glass box, on display, for your people to come and stare at your mummy for small change? How would you feel about it?

Here is a letter from Mr. Samir, director of the "Atlantis oil healing centre"

When Julia arrived to my healing centre, "Atlantis", I was not surprised. I was waiting for her. I saw a dream during the night that someone from the royal Pharaohs' family would visit me in the morning and would bring some special gift to Egypt. I felt the unusual energy from this gift. She did bring a gift for the Big Pyramid. It was a special rock from Chichen Itza, from the famous Mexican pyramid!

Julia told me that for years in her dreams some ancient person, a priest or pharaoh talked to her from Egypt. She described this person in detail and the animal which accompanied him, and she told me that they have a very special relationship. I know instantly that this animal was Anubis. I explained to her that this was a mixed breed of dog and fox in Egypt, and each pharaoh had his own animal which lived with him during his lifetime, and followed him after death to the other side to protect him there. The Man with a very long head was possibly Akhenaton, Nephertiti's husband. He is the only one we know who had this shape of head.

I felt that she had a very unusual, powerful energy within her. She mentioned that the next day she was going inside the big Cheops pyramid. I instantly felt responsible for her preparation to this event. I felt it was necessary to have her undergo "an oil session" according to the ancient Egyptian tradition. It felt that some High Power or God sent me to help her to make the necessary adjustments for the special meeting with the Spirits of Ancient Egypt. So I had an "oil session" numerous times with her. The result was astonishing!

The next day and the following day she told me in details what happened to her after my sessions. She also started asking me about a very magic, unusual cat, which was visiting her! A blue-colored cat. I knew instantly that this was the Holy Spirit of Bast, the Royal Cat Goddess, which visits only very highly spiritual people. And maybe only once in a life time! This is a very rare gift. Julia was very lucky. And I am proud of my involvement to this story.

Amelia Reborn? Egypt

Samir Ali Baba, Egyptian healer, "Atlantis centre", Giza, Egypt[16] *[3]*

Mr. Samir with his oil machine

Mr. Samir and his staff kindly offered to me an oil chakras' massage. He has a big collection of organic oils with wonderful fragrances made from all kinds of plants, flowers and seeds. His place looks like a crystal

---

[16] Efir oils acquired such a name because of their ability to influence the thinnest, invisible energy cover of the human body-auras. Efir is something impossible to touch or see or feel. The same is true of the Efir oil; it is impossible to touch, see or measure its quality. The influence of the Efir oil is on the level of the invisible, untouchable and unconscious feelings. People use Efir oil as an energy food for the consciousness, not on the physical but on the energy level. It works on the mind. It is much more powerful than logic or rational thinking. The process used in the treatment, called aromatherapy, means treatment by plant fragrance, and this term was introduce by the French partum designer, Rene Mari Gattefos.

kingdom with thousands of oil canisters and containers. The containers were of all sizes and colors and some looked like Christmas tree ornaments. When I saw all these treasures, I started remembering my childhood.

I ended up swimming in these oils! I was covered from head to toe, totally submerged in fragrant oils. It was an absolutely fabulous feeling bathing in this oil bath! I returned to the hotel in my Japanese kimono smelling like a bunch of exotic flowers with the aura of this luxury fragrance surrounding me.

I was delayed to go to bed, almost until midnight. It was the end of my first day in Egypt. I had arrived very late the night before and got up early in the morning to see the pyramids, so now I was trying to organize my stuff and thoughts a little bit....

The Oil Decanters

When I turned off the light I found that my room was overcrowded with all these Egyptian "papyrus animals"! It was very sudden and unexpected... I was scared, maybe for the first time in my whole life! I turned the light on instantly and closed my eyes. But I continued seeing them! So I tried to keep my eyes open..., but I was very sleepy. So I repeated the exercise – closed and opened, closed and opened, like in a hide-and-seek game.... They were real live Spirits! They were a little bit shorter than normal people. All of them wore masks! All of them were in my room! A full set of Egyptian "papyrus drawings" were standing in my hotel room! They seemed to be saying, "Finally she is going to bed and our time has started!"

At one point one of them stood very close to me. That was Anubis – and he bent down over my face. Another one touched the big toe of each of my feet, pinching it slightly, very fast and at the same moment, he touched the place where the third eye should be – in the middle of the forehead. This creature, Spirit..., stayed near the end of the bed where my feet were. How it can be possible that I started feeling my third eye at the same time? I just couldn't explain it.... [6] It looked like this Spirit was trying to make some adjustments; activate my energy flow through the channels and my third eye vision. Nonetheless, I soon fell asleep with the little light near my bed and the red, elegant lamp in the corner on.

In my dream, I saw myself sitting in a big chair – a throne – with all these animals down and around me.... They were talking to me in this unusual, bird-like voices..., kind of asking how I had been all these years?... As if I was meeting them again after a very long absence while traveling far away....
I know now, without any doubt, that this oil massage, this fragrant oil bath was the key! It was a very

important and necessary step for these spirits to recognize me and accept me as part of their environment. It was important also that it happened before I visited the tomb the following day. I knew then that the oil bath was an important ritual.

Plants play a very important role here. Time goes on, but exactly the same kind of plants grows around here, the same kinds that grew in Egypt thousands of years ago. These oils from the Egyptian plants helped my spirit reconnect with the Egyptian spirits and with my past! Maybe it was also an ancient tradition to be soaked in this oil. Maybe this way, the oils penetrated the skin very deeply and influenced the chakras, aura, spirit level..., or I don't know how to name all of this – which we can not see or touch, but is still a part of us.

There was something else that became part of the ritual – and which is part of us. During the oil sessions, Mr. Samir sang some ancient Egyptian song and prayed with a low vibrato in his voice. I started seeing myself inside some room with huge solid walls and because of the very long, but not wide window that was very deep, I could feel the heat from outside and I saw the white desert sand in the distance. I saw him talking to me that time in a room and I understood what he said, and I caught myself talking back to him in this ancient Egyptian language....

In my second dream, I saw myself sitting inside some big, golden box near the pyramid. The pyramid was two-third complete; only the last third part on the top was still unfinished. There was a big fan, slowly moving round and round, on my right side and I saw people working on huge rocks on the left side of me. A man with long painted eyes was sitting next to me on my left and talking slowly.... He had black hair, cut straight across the forehead, tanned skin, and he wore some unusual, shiny, blue and gold striped fabric covering his head and both sides of it. I saw that his hand was covered with some symbols, drawings....

My next dream was a global dream where past and present societies meet in the desert near the pyramids in that area. Someone teaches me in my dream and I received four lessons.

Close to the morning, I saw something extremely magic! I am not sure that I was still asleep or already awake; it was in between, because I heard the sounds of the birds outside on that big tree, full of orange flowers near my patio....

The "Cat" stood on the floor in the middle of my bathroom! It pushed the bathroom door with his paw and opened it, but I remained inside and it looked at me with his round, shiny, huge eyes. He had the smoothest, silkiest fur I could ever imagine. I am not sure about his color, maybe it was black or very dark blue, but his fur was very shiny with bright blue, turquoise intense reflection in it. It was astonishingly beautiful!

I woke up that morning with a strong feeling. I felt one point at the back of my head, where the crown chakra and pineal gland are located, and I am sure this was also influenced by those oils, or maybe the pyramids, which were very close to the hotel.

I remember when I lived in the Korean Buddhist temple, a few years ago, I had the same feeling of this point; I could feel it continually when I was there. I also felt the place between the eyebrows – the third eye chakra – at the back of the eyes, located near hypothalamus and pituitary glands. In the Korean temple; I also felt that point between the upper lip and the nose.

On the way to breakfast I stopped near the window of a papyrus store in the hotel lobby. This little store was not open yet. But to my big surprise, I saw my night-guest on display! Exactly the same, a beautiful, blue cat! It was a drawing on a papyrus!

Bast, the Royal Cat Goddess

On the opposite wall, I saw some drawing representing a scene with all of these Egyptian Goddesses and animals, the same personages which visited me in my room and in my dream the previous night!

"Judgment day" with all Egyptian animal Goddesses

Later that day, I asked Mr. Samir about the cat. He told me that I was very lucky that this cat visited me. Her name is Bast, the Royal Cat Goddess, a royal cat, which visits very spiritual people sometimes. He told me that the cat will come again and will be closer each time. He was absolutely right. (Read below what happened the next day, in the afternoon!)

As for me, I know for sure that I was not asleep yet when I started seeing all of these Egyptian Spirit animals. I also heard the birds chirping in the morning when I saw the cat. Mr. Samir told me that this Spirit cat lives around the pyramids and visits people from time to time. Now I am really confused – He is a Spirit, right? He is not a real live cat.... I am still a scientist and I wish to have some explanation of this mystery.

I thought about it during the next few days and even now this cat still comes to my mind from time to time. I bought a little statue of him and he is right in front of me, right now, watching....

I know when people think about ghosts; these entities feed on people's energy, especially on their fear. Fear makes the ghosts stronger and they can even start moving objects or harm people.... Maybe it's the same story with this cat? Maybe it was the spirit of an ordinary cat a long time ago walking around, but people's thoughts are material and ultimately they created this beautiful blue-color cat in their imagination? And now this image, this phantom DNA, is moving around and some spiritual people who can see energy see him as well?

The problem was that I never knew this cat existed until I saw it with my own eyes or perhaps, I should say, I saw him with my feelings....

Maybe it was the same story with this Egyptian Goddess and animals. A long time ago they were real people with masks; later people reproduced their images in paintings, on papyruses, and in the statues. So they always had these people in mind and it continued for thousands of years.... Ultimately, their images became strong enough that ordinary people, like me, could see them in profile, or feel them at the stage when they're about to fall asleep or were not fully awake yet.[17]

This twilight zone, by the way, this in-between stage of not being asleep and being asleep always brought me many visions during my life.

And now back to the cat subject. I remember that last year, in August, I was sitting silently with my daughter on the porch at the back of the house in Kauai. We

---

[17] In Tibetan Buddhism, magical practices involved creating "tylpas" known in Western occultism as thought-form. Typlas, thought-forms, are imaginary entities that can be given energy and artificial life through rituals, meditation, and other workings. The poet W.B. Yeats started a magical order in which he tried to revive certain Celtic deities through visualizations and ceremonies. One of them, the "white jester", apparently gained enough independent vitality to become visible to few of Yeast's friends, who were not aware of what he was doing. Daniel Pinchbeck, 2012 The return of Quetzalcoatl, 2006.

returned from the beach and we were very relaxed.... Suddenly she asked me, "Did you see that cat?" I replied instantly, "Of course I saw him!" But when I turned to the side and looked at the place where the cat had been sitting, it was no longer there! It did not exist! I could continue seeing it from the corner of my eye, but could not see it if I looked straight at it! It was the spirit of the cat, which may have lived there at one time and was now visiting this place.

Anyway, let's return to Egypt and the days I spent there.

It was a very special and important morning for me. It was the day I needed to run to the pyramid ASAP! As early as possible! My goal was to be the first person to visit the tomb inside the pyramid! They only sell a hundred tickets a day. We were the very first with Mohamed to arrive. Our car was first in line, we bought the ticket first and I ran directly to the entrance. The guards called me Shakira and started telling me not to be afraid, because I was going first and that I would be totally alone inside....

I just shoved my way passed them and I didn't pay any attention to their words. At first, it was a solid entrance leading into a wide corridor. All of the walls were made of strong, giant, granite rocks, but soon it turned into a very narrow corridor, a small tunnel like a square mouse hole. This corridor went up and up, and up and I couldn't see or know what I would find at the end of it, in the dark!

It was so narrow that two people abreast could not move through it – I think. I was glad that there were some electrical lights in there... I could imagine how difficult and uncomfortable it would have been for someone in ancient times to move through this narrow hole with a torch in one hand and carrying all these ritual tools in the other.... There would not be much oxygen to breathe with the torches burning – because there are no windows; it is deep inside the pyramid. In order to go through, you have to climb and crawl through this tunnel. Instead of steps there are just metal staples.... You can not stand straight; you need to move up by climbing in a bent or sitting position with a very narrow, rocky ceiling extending above you. I advise people, who have claustrophobia, never, ever to go there; you would be scared to death.

Well..., I was glad when it was over and I could stand straight and walk again.... Finally, I was inside this big room with a high ceiling. It was dark in there; you could hardly see the sarcophagus near the opposite wall. But for some reason I was very excited and happy to be there alone! No word to describe it! It was like a dream come true and here I was!

First, I gave a present to the Great Cheops pyramid; my special present from my precious crystal, my Mexican Chichen Itza pyramid. I hid it in the most important place and far from the guard's eye, the one who would come, and clean the place. I felt strongly about the importance of this, it was like a ritual and now it was done, completed. Next, I did what doctor Alfons taught me. I said aloud to the top of my voice: "I am not more than somebody else, I am not less than somebody else, I am myself." And then I pronounced all my reincarnations one by one: Queen from Atlantis, woman with a crown from Egypt, Priest Jaguar, Magician from Chichen Itza, pilot Amelia from USA, T. from Tibet, and Julia & Jasmine Rose from Canada, Svadihatra, a human from the future".

The sound was extremely strong, bright and very loud. Each word continued to echo many, many times.... It was like a symphony orchestra with drums and gongs. Wow! I loved it! This sound was great! Wow! Wow! Wow!

Suddenly something changed.... At first, for a second, I was frozen and silent. Next, I started talking in some unusual language! I just talked quietly, as if I was praying. I didn't have any control over what was going on with me.... I did not feel my body, my muscles or bones; there was just one pillar of energy going up through my body. I finished with some strange movement, as if I was performing some rite, with strange bends; up and down and to the side. It felt the same as if Chi Gong energy was pulling me in different directions. I was like a toy, a puppet in someone's invisible hands. I felt as if I were in heaven with this carrying, cuddling energy within and around me. I ended up leaning with my back toward the sarcophagus and both arms spread wide to the sides of the top of the sarcophagus's wall. I was facing the entrance on the opposite side, in total silence, when I started hearing an echo from down below; up through the corridor, and moments later, three Japanese tourists entered the room. One of the women was suddenly scared to death. She was screaming, literally jumped, and ran to her husband. I guess she saw someone (me) – a dark human shape – near the sarcophagus and decided that I was a ghost....

It was a problem to return outside, by the way. As usual, I took control of the situation. First, I asked the Japanese tourists who already came up to the room to wait until the second group would come up, through the narrow corridor, so that we could have a free passage to return one by one down the staples, down the corridor and out of the pyramid. Then, I sent this first group of tourists through this corridor and stopped to wait for the next group down below to arrive until the corridor was cleared out. I was glad that they were Japanese tourists because they fully cooperated and did exactly what I asked them to do. I am not sure what it would have been if instead of Japanese I would have been faced with a bunch of spoiled American teens, for example. I think it would have been a nightmare and we would have all been "entombed" there forever....

After the pyramid, I went to visit the Sphinx that morning. By the way, at the Sphinx, I experienced the strongest sensation I had while visiting Egypt. I felt waves of goose bumps going up and down my body continually. One local boy ran to me and offered to show me an ancient wall with real Egyptian hieroglyphs, the statue of King Ramses II and so on. I ran with him through the desert and to the ruins. My driver was waiting in the car far away where the first street into town starts. When I ran back, passing the Sphinx, right at the entrance, I found myself face to face with that Japanese family. The man told me, "It was a good idea for you to bring a flash light!"

I looked at him and just didn't understand what he meant. I asked him to repeat, "What did you say?"

He then told me that when they entered the room, at the back of me and around me, there was a glowing light, like an aura from the flashlight which I kept at my back... and when I left it was gone! How could that be? I did not have any flash light! And I remember that my hands were spread on both sides of the sarcophagus.... When I told him that I didn't have any flashlight, he also remembered not seeing a torch in my hand, and instantly began to step away from me – walking backwards.... That was all really strange: this Japanese family and what they saw or didn't see. At first, the wife was scared to death, which could possibly be explained in the darken room, but now the husband seemed in shock when he realized that I didn't carry a flashlight...and stepped away from me – in broad daylight.... I guess they were exhausted after climbing that scary corridor. Anyway, he gave me a good idea – next time I will take a flashlight with me.

The next morning I became aware of "new" muscles in my legs – the muscles in front of my legs from my knees upward. I think people never use these muscles in their entire life! I found out, the hard way, that I have them when I could hardly stand up or try to walk – I was in great pain. It continued to be painful for more than a week. Even when I left Egypt and I was back in Canada, my legs continued aching. I walked like a handicapped person or a very old grandmother....

I remember giving one of my paintings for an exhibition; it was at the time I was at the university. I received many compliments..., but my painting was stolen! It looks like someone liked it way too much. I should have made a scan from it, but who could expect that a painting would disappear from a university exhibition?

It is interesting that I always loved the desert. I often drew pictures of deserts, palm trees, camels. In Egypt, near the pyramids I saw exactly the same shapes with my own eyes – for real! I was very happy and excited!

By the way, near the pyramids, I saw two models from Malaysia. We even took a few good shots together near the Sphinx. One girl had her hair styled as the Priest from Chichen Itza had sometimes! I was stunned when I saw it from the back – it was exactly the same shape and how his hair was combed. The Priest also wore his hair in a pony-tail sometimes. His hair was long and thick and he had all kinds of hair styles.

Here is a photo of that girl from the back.

Malaysian model in Egypt the Priest's hair style

That day, I had a second oil bath in the evening, and the Spirits visited me again! This time, I was in bed, ready to take an afternoon nap, not under the influence of the oils, like the first time, not in the darken room, only the curtains were drawn to shade the room from the sunlight. It was the middle of the day!

This part is very interesting....

131

Amelia Reborn? Egypt

I was again in the "twilight zone", right before I fell asleep. I was lying down on my back, in my comfy "5-star-bed", sinking into the softest pillows with my hands lying on my tummy. Suddenly, I saw the blue cat on the floor near my bed! He jumped up and landed softly on top of my hands. I stopped breathing... It was the softest, warmest ball of energy. The cat was sitting and looking directly into my face. I could see his eyes, with the lines across the eyes – in detail! It was hilarious.... The cat continued to sit for the next two or three minutes, when, from the corner of my eye, I saw this Anubis, the Spirit animal, which stood near the next empty bed! He stood like a human at first, in his Fox and Dog mask... but, as soon as I saw him, he bent slowly and slid instantly from a standing position to a lying down one on top of that bed! He lay down as dogs usually lie down and looked the way he does in many of his statues. It was truly amazing; it was a wave of pure energy! I saw something like this in a movie, in a computer animation maybe – when robots turn from one configuration into another. Or when the Chi Gong master moves like a wave... I fell asleep instantly after this, and I don't remember anything else.

BUT this "movement" got top points in my book of all the magic things I experienced in this truly Mysterious Egypt. Egypt is now like a jewelry box for me which if you would open it, you would be astonished seeing the flush of rare, magic multicolored things inside it.

This animal Anubis, I saw it twice in Chichen Itza in the temple on the top of the pyramid during my past life reading. It was during the sacrifice scene. Then I saw him the first evening when all these Egyptian animal Goddesses visited me. He was always near me that night and now he showed up again!

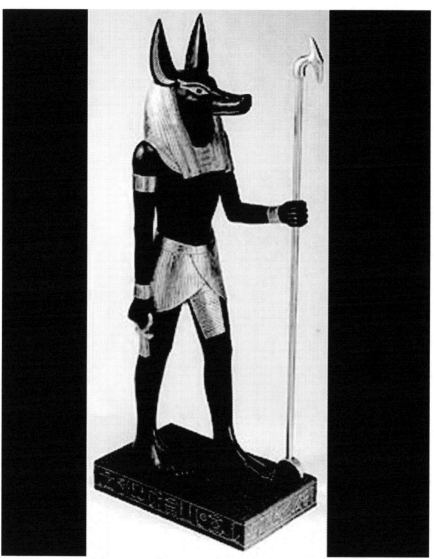

Anubis standing . . . beside the empty bed

Anubis lying down [5]

When I woke up that afternoon, I continued lying down with closed eyes for a few seconds, and suddenly, I had a vision. It was very fast, like a flash, like in the blink of an eye, but I remember it.

I saw two giants with crowds of normal size people around them. There were about 40 or 50 people there, the top of their heads only reaching the hips of the giants. All of them, including the giants, were wearing luxurious, beautiful, very ornate outfits. This crowd was standing where today the road from the Cheops pyramid to the second big pyramid crosses the road going to the Sphinx....

For some reason, each time we drove through this area, I always found an excuse to ask the driver to stop the

134

car at that place – to take a photo or to see a policeman on the camel or something else. I always wanted to stop there and step outside the car for a little bit; something invisible attracted me to that spot. I felt something really unusual there. I saw this place in my vision, but at a different angle. Maybe this place marked our Stargate to the past?

People who read this passage may say: "At first she saw a big man in Mexico, now she sees giant people in Egypt!" Yes, I saw a huge man in Mexico with many little details of his daily life and he was a dear friend of mine. And yes, I saw these two giants for a short moment in that area at the crossroads from the pyramids to the Sphinx. What can I do about it? Yes, I saw them and I trust my vision very much, since throughout my life what I saw and felt has come true and happened. I saw, in my vision, a blue, pink, and yellow round sphere near the pyramids while I was in the plane, even before I arrived in Egypt. I wrote it in my little book in the plane to check my record later, and I saw them right there, on the first morning I arrived, right near the pyramid! While I am typing this, I am thinking now about these two giants... maybe they were Atlantis people, too? And I remember that the tour guide mentioned that near the Sphinx they found the *Hall of Records* which Atlantis people left ... and that Edgar Cayce mentioned this in his predictions.

Edgar Cayce – Atlantean Hall of Records

Edgar Cayce predicted the discovery of an Atlantean "Hall of Records" between the Sphinx and the Nile with a connecting entrance under the right, front paw of the Sphinx.

The following segment was taken from Cayce, Edgar "On Atlantis" New York: Warner Books, 1968.

Amelia Reborn? Egypt

...It would be well if this entity were to seek either of the three phases of the ways and means in which those records of the activities of individuals were preserved – the one in the Atlantean land, that sank, which will rise and is rising again; another in the place of the records that leadeth from the Sphinx to the hall of records, in the Egyptian land; and another in the Aryan or Yucatan land, where the temple there is overshadowing same, (2012-1; Sep 25, 1939).

...the entity joined with those who were active in putting the records in forms that were partially of the old characters of the ancient or early Egyptian, and part in the newer form of the Atlanteans. These may be found, especially when the house or tomb of records is opened, in a few years from now, (2537-1; Jul 17, 1941).

[The entity] was among the first to set the records that are yet to be discovered or yet to be had of those activities in the Atlantean land, and for the preservation of data that is yet to be found from the chambers of the way between the Sphinx and the pyramid of records, (3575-2; Jan 20, 1944) – p.147.

A record of Atlantis from the beginning of those periods when the Spirit took form, or began the encasements in that land; and the developments of the peoples throughout their sojourn; together with the record of the first destruction, and the changes that took place in the land; with the record of the sojourning of the peoples and their varied activities in other lands, and a record of the meetings of all the nations or lands, for the activities in the destruction of Atlantis; and the building of the pyramid of initiation, together with whom, what, and where the opening of the records would come, that are as copies from the sunken Atlantis. For with the change, it [Atlantis] must rise again. In position, this lies – as the sun

136

rises from the waters – as the line of the shadows (or light) falls between the paws of the Sphinx; that was set later as the sentinel or guard and which may not be entered from the connecting chambers from the Sphinx's right paw until the time has been fulfilled when the changes must be active in this sphere of man's experience. Then [it lies] between the Sphinx and the river (378-16; Oct 29, 1933) – P.147-8 (*On Atlantis – New York: Warner Books, 1968*).

WOW! Today, June 22, 2008 – 3:45 p.m. when I almost finished the book and I was only checking pictures; I suddenly found a website about Giants in Egypt!! Giant-Titan Pharaoh!

You cannot compare the brilliant Edgar Cayce's predictions and feelings about the tall Atlanteans when you can see them in your own eyes on the real ancient picture! And it is exactly what I saw in my vision!

Egyptian Giant-Titan Pharaoh

The photo shows a Titan Pharaoh of Egypt with typical red-ochre skin paint. The Titans were the Adanyas, and settled in the British Isles and the Americas. They and others were called them 'Red Men' because of their red-ochre painted skin.

What really struck me: this is extra proof that I can go back to 2,000 years in Mexico or 7,000 years in Egypt and see, really see, how people lived in those times. And it is obvious to me that during those times giant people were living and walking this Earth amid normal-size people.

But it is also an additional proof that the CAT and Anubis were real "spirits" which I could see (and feel) in my vision.

It shows amazing possibilities to us "mere human beings"! It feels as if there is a storage of information somewhere – a library of lives.
So, who you are right now, what you do, will be stored in that library and people in the future will have the possibility to see you in their past!

****

I am very excited right now and overwhelmed. I even allowed myself to visit the kitchen and eat cherries and ginger in chocolate, right before dinner. I love sour cherries very much! The black Golden Cat Bastet and Anubis are hiding and staring at me through the jasmine and roses on my desk. The nearby vase is full of white, I daisies. At this moment, I am in Heaven!

I sent this letter to Egypt yesterday...

Happy to hear from you, dear Samir!

Magic things continue to happen to me in Canada.

The Spirit Cat visited me again during my dream. It was right after I returned home. I was tired after the flight and I was deep asleep for a long time, so I don't remember the details.

But what happened today was really amazing. Today is June 12 – 5:30p.m. I decided to take a nap for an hour. I asked my daughter to wake me up at 6:30p.m. I lay down in bed, closed my eyes and as soon as I did, I saw a girl right near me. Her face was very close to me. I wasn't even asleep yet. While I continued looking at this face, I heard my daughter opening the entrance door and taking her bike outside.

This girl has the face of a doll, with big eyes, full lips and full cheeks – kind of a baby look, puffy. She has an ebony face with a very smooth skin. A powder or sand-spray of bright, lapis-lazuli color seemed to be sprayed over her ebony face! She was too perfect to be human. She was a Spirit – or I don't know how to name it. At first, I thought that maybe she was the Spirit Cat who decided to show himself as a girl – or maybe the opposite – maybe she showed herself as a cat to people, but she was really the Spirit of a girl, because she had this neon-blue color powder covering this smoothest ebony skin. She continued to peer down at me with this very serious look in her eye. I just didn't know what to do! For a moment, I thought that even she has this black face, she is not a person from Africa, although this black color was not painted on her face. I know that she is from Egypt, but she has also a kind of Persian look.... When I was thinking about her looks, it reminded me of the Tutankhamen mask. It had the same features – of the

139

same nationality. I thought that maybe she is not even a girl – maybe she is a boy. Perhaps, I brought her spirit from Egypt with me and now she lives here? Or maybe, while I was in Egypt, the Spirits began to know that I could see them and now they visit me and show themselves to me! I continued looking at her and she continued staring at me – I just didn't know what to do next.

I decided to check if it was my imagination or if I was seeing a real Spirit. I decided to ask her some questions; suddenly I had so many things to ask. So I stood up and went to my desk, took a pen and paper to write down the answers. While I was preparing myself for this "interview", she disappeared. So, I went back to bed and fell asleep. When my daughter woke me up, I thought that maybe this was one of my dreams. How can it be possible? Yet, when I looked near me, I saw the pen and paper, which I brought to bed when I saw her before I fell asleep!

It looks like after your amazing oil baths, I saw Spirits in Egypt many times, so many times in fact, that I started getting used to them as if it was normal – part of my daily routine! So today, instead of being surprised, I just enjoyed looking at her and maybe asked something simple – I am already way too practical! I am sure that she is still here and that I would see her as soon as I closed my eyes. I am sure she is not the ghost of some dead person. She looked very radiant, healthy and beautiful and way too perfect to be human. She was astonishingly beautiful! Who is she? Do you know maybe?

Sincerely,

Julia

PS:

The same thing happened to me once before – a few years after my mother died. I saw her in my dreams sometimes and talked to her. I decided to check if I was talking with my real mother or if this was just a dream. I decided to ask her, next time, something real and see if it would come true. I know that people, after death, know the future, because they are in another dimension. So, at that time, before going to sleep, (again it was my afternoon nap) I asked my mother to tell me the numbers for the 6/49 lottery. I knew the lottery results were only a few hours away – the same day. I never played any lottery before, but this time it would help me receiving an answer. In my dream, I saw my mother; she stood before me and smiled. Next, she started lifting numbers with a little handle, one by one, on a standard size of white paper.

I often remember myself in my dream. So as soon as I realized that this was a dream, and my mother was answering my question, I woke up instantly – amazed! I woke up after the fourth number. I decided then to check the results and went to the store. And YES, I had four winning numbers! Well, if I knew this beforehand, for sure, I should have bought nine more tickets, chosen the next 5 numbers – one by one, and I would have won $60,000 on that day. Yet more important to me than winning the lottery, was the fact that I knew my real mother had come to me in my dream!

This is why I decided today to ask this girl about something real, as well. Anyway, I ran trying to find a container, some vase, or an amphora to accommodate her Spirit. Somehow, I knew instantly what to do since I have a connection with the Priest! Lucky that I found a brand new, fine quality "porcelain" vase from China.

Amelia Reborn? Egypt

From Samir:

You should know that you have with you good spirits from Egypt and you should have more of my oils to keep you communicating with them, it is very important. I know you are a very good and highly spiritual person.

Then I started to study this mystic cat and girl. Here is what I found.

Bastet

Responsible For: Joy, Music, and Dancing! Also Health and Healing. She also protected humans against contagious diseases and evil spirits. Her cult can be traced back to about 3200 BC, and she became a national deity when Bubastis became the capital of Egypt in about 950 BC.

If you plan to do a portrayal of Bastet, consider wearing a red costume – a priestess of Bastet, like the goddess herself, was known as "the Lady with the Red Clothes" http://www.shira.net/egypt-goddess.htm.

By the way, it was said that this priestess of Bastet was like the goddess herself and was known as "the Lady with the Red Clothes". For some unexplained reason I brought a red dress with gold ornament with me to Egypt and started wearing this red dress during the next two days after I saw the Bastet Cat, when I visited the pyramid and the Sphinx and until I left Egypt. Now I know why! It was my intuition in the first place that told me take this dress, and after I met the cat I started wearing that dress because it suited this situation perfectly, according to ancient Egyptian rules!

When I read this, I understand who this extremely beautiful girl was. She is the Goddess, the Spirit that came to me in the middle of the day and showed herself as soon as I closed my eyes! She is the Goddess priestess of Bastet! I was not sleeping; I was 100% awake! She appeared immediately after I close my eyes. Moreover, she was not a ghost. She is a real live Goddess in Spirit world and comes in our world since I saw her.

I found more about Bast and now I know why this is all connected with the perfume oils! Wow!

Bast, Perfumed Protector, Cat Goddess

Her name has the hieroglyph of a 'bas'-jar with the feminine ending of 't'. These jars were heavy perfume jars, often filled with expensive perfumes – they were very valuable in Egypt, considering the Egyptian need (with the hot weather) of makeup, bathing, hygiene and (of course) perfume. Bast, by her name, seems to be related to perfumes in some way. Her son Nefertem, a solar god, was a god of perfumes and alchemy, which supports the theory.
http://www.crystalinks.com/bast.html

It is an endless pleasure to look at her beauty! On top of an absolutely black skin, she has a dark, very bright, blue color – something like the *"neon fish"* I saw in a pet store. It is exactly the same as the Cat had on top of his black-colored fur – this bright, neon blue color! This is why I was sure that they were connected somehow. Now I know that these are actually two Spirits in one – such as I saw myself many times, in my dreams, as a twin.

So this Anubis, which came to me and slid down from one position to another, and the Cat, which came already three times, and this Goddess girl – all of them

143

are REAL and exist in our world! And I will be very happy to meet them again!

It is interesting to note that all of them are as black as ebony and that their statues are all sprayed with gold. Maybe 7,000 years ago the sun emitted very strong radiation, or for some other reason, people and animals at the time were black.

From another side, totally black color will not have any reflection and it will be impossible to see it! Wow! Maybe this is the way how this goddess is hiding in our world between us? So we can see them only in special condition. Those scientists, who will create this kind of fabric, will be geniuses!

Bast, Perfumed Protector, Cat Goddess

I can tell you a secret that may help you to see them. First, you need to divest yourself from stress, get out from a negative environment and away from negative people. Since they are never happy with themselves, they will always try to control you, ensuring that your door to happiness is locked as well. The problem with people is that they don't like and don't want you to change. They will try to shut you down. It is also best to disconnect your TV, where they always show negative news, and all your wireless equipment[18] which kills your psychic ability and may ruin your health. Instead, spend time with plants and nature. Eat only when you're hungry and just a little amount to give your body a rest from toxins and the possibility to return to health fast while being in excellent shape physically and mentally.

YES! But you should already have a happy disposition, be optimistic, and spiritual with only very positive, kindest, pure, direct from the heart, loving the whole world kind of thoughts. Some "oil sessions" with

---

[18] Regarding wireless equipment – since the fall of 2007 bees have begun to die in great numbers in the USA and Europe. In the western US states, 60%, and in the eastern states 70% of bees have disappeared. In Europe it also happened in Germany, Spain, Portugal, Switzerland, Italy, and Greece. Scientists from Landau University in Germany found that in most cases the electromagnetic waves of the wireless phones and antennas destroyed the mechanism of the orientation in the bee's body, and the bees simply couldn't find their way home! No bees, no harvest. Most of the people who are using cell phones don't know that they are not only killing bees, they are killing themselves as well – and fast. Soon there will be NO food. Many people will then start remembering that Albert Einstein told us that people could only survive for a few years after the bees will have disappeared.

It is my most sincere wish that people who read this book would stop using their cell phones, except in case of emergency. By the way, cell phones can also cook brain cells in the same way as if you were to put your brain in a microwave.

someone like Mr. Samir from Egypt may help a lot as well.

Soon this effort will pay off. It will open doors for you to see amazing dreams, to connect with wise Spirits and receive lessons from powerful giant Gods and Goddesses.

The Mystery of the Sahara and the Pyramids

This is a statue of a woman Sphinx
I was attracted to her and could not stop staring at her.

Amelia's smile...?
Do you see a resemblance in her features with those of Amelia's?

Dream # 3
CROWN, September 6, 1991

Maybe there were many people; maybe the Lord was speaking. It was a very long and serious dream. Something was going to happen to me, something they were all waiting for. Everybody stood in their places, each in his or her own alcove – designed for just one person. There were men to the one side of me and women to the other. I started to wave my hands, like a butterfly. Then I looked at myself from above, as if a huge creature was looking down onto little ants – The Power!

Two girls took me by the arms. They came to stand at my side at once. Some wave-like process started – very energetic, very dense – maybe it was a cloud. It seemed I had seen it in my dream already. I was entering this wave, and someone was moving my body, as if in the wind, very powerfully, without my participation. It was becoming stronger. The girls were holding my upper arms with one hand and joined their other hand to form a circle. I remember hanging my head downward. I saw my hair, very thick, ash-blond, running in a wave motion down to the floor. Their hair was also very long – chestnut or black – touching the ground. It was waving in the same rhythm. I don't remember what happened afterwards.

I felt like a caterpillar turning into a butterfly. I understood that it had happened, and then they seated me on something and carried me somewhere. I was sitting at level with their heads. Then I lay down in a recumbent position. I saw a sign written above someone's head – something most important – the goal. The man was sitting on an eminence's throne – five steps up from the floor of the hall. This hall was made of marble surrounded by columns. He had a beard and long hair. He was performing some enchanting, powerful acts, ignoring the others. He looked very noble, dressed in white, pleated robes like a God.... I saw a sign in the space. It was very important; this was the most important thing in my dream – like hieroglyphs, in which the Chinese see a lot of meaning. It was a complex sign, a round sphere, and inside it, some inscription which reflected all of the essence of the disciples as a whole. Any person, who does not know anything, after looking at this sign, could have understood everything, not through their intellect but through their "perception". Then there was a chasm.... There were high columns which were dividing the space into segments. Men were on the left of me; women on the right. The left side was more important. I was in the center. Something was happening.... When I remember this later on, I had seen a sphere in front of me, then I had seen myself from above, and on my head there was an oval-shaped, very clear cut hole – straight through the occipital membrane – ready to insert the crystal. Inside – the eternity, like in space. It was much unexpected. I raised my eyes and saw another hemisphere.

Later, I saw a red cap of the same form as the concave shape in front of me and I wanted very much to put it on. I was impatient, but they gave it to me instantly and I put it on. It was covered with crystals, large stones.... One of the girls, when she noticed my impatience, giggled, as if saying, "You'll get it anyway!" It was incredibly comfortable and it fitted exactly, although there were no strings or laces, but it fitted tightly. The hemisphere was round at the base, but on the top, it turned into a pyramid with a square-cut top.

Next they placed the second, spherical hat on top of the conical.

Nefertiti

What is in her head? It looks like a cut pyramid, square at the bottom, like what I saw in my dream. Can anyone tell me?

The figure on the next page is what I drew, right after I woke up. She may be the girl from Egypt, but also maybe from Atlantis. She had a small kind of hole in the scalp like the Priest had. So I decided to put these three dreams together. This subject with the hole in the scalp was repeated many times in different dreams.

Girl with a crown, from the dream dated, September 6, 1991

PS:
The mystery was solved when I visited the Cairo museum in May 2008. I found, the mystery was solved when I visited the Cairo museum in May 2008. I found, among many others, two sarcophagi which had exactly the same "crown" on their heads that I saw and put on my own head in my dream after this special ritual! It was the shape of a cut pyramid with a square bottom which is the same shape as the Chichen Itza pyramid, by the way. I asked the opinion of three representatives in the museum and they all went with me to see these "crowns". They all told me that this is the symbol of royalty; it is a queen's crown! What an unusual shape!

It looks like, in my dream, I was the subject of a royal initiation ritual. This could explain why I was so attached to the mummies in the Cairo museum, why I had goose bumps, why I was looking for the house where I lived before, and why I was so angry that the mummies had been removed from the pyramids. Maybe, in my past life, I was one of the royalties who later was entombed and removed to the museum room. For all these answers I need to visit the wise Di Cherry again and ask her to read these dreams....

Today, I found one more dream, it was 16 years ago.

Dream # 4
The Fox and the Sarcophagus, February 23, 1992

(Unfortunately, I lost the first page with the beginning, of this dream)

After that, I saw the Fox who sat on a stone, with a long nose and long ears, like a monument, a statue, on a rectangular box which stood on two gold spheres. Below, there is a grotto, an entrance. Through this secret entrance there is a key – moving the rectangular box – spheres. Below this entrance there is the tomb of a queen, a sarcophagus. In the front of it there are two hieroglyphs (the same as on the rectangular box of the Fox). Under the sarcophagus, there are stone tiles with inscriptions. There are four signs: an ibis..., and some pictures of a yellow crown, the large lizard, beads – six pieces (the beads are similar to fireballs, lightning fire bolts).

****

I did not know in 1992 that the FOX actually had the name of Anubis and I had not decoded the name yet. I believe this was my own sarcophagus. I saw this place numerous times in my dreams and wanted to find it....

I couldn't put here the full information of what was written on the sarcophagus. One day I might go to try to find my own tomb in Egypt. Maybe it is somewhere in Sakkara, among hundreds of pyramids, where the sarcophagi of kings, priests and their families are laid to rest. Sakkara is located about 30 miles from Giza.

Regarding Nefertiti, I found the original statue in the Cairo museum. Workers in the museum told me that YES, what she was wearing was indeed a crown which was placed on her head after the statue was carved. But around the crown should be part of her head. The bust is not complete or has been broken.

Today, a week later, I found this information, and below, on the photo, you'll see exactly the shape of the hat and crown I saw in my dream!

Conical Hats Worn By Gods

http://www.crystalinks.com/conicalhats.html.
http://members.aol.com/marslandsr/hats.htm.
God and Goddesses and Quetzalcoatl all wear a conical cap such as the wind god Ehecatl. He brought love into the world by mating with the maid Mayahuel as a single tree with flowering branch.

****

In my dream, at the end, they placed the second, spherical hat on top of the conical.

The two hats – the conical and the spherical

Cretan goddess, young, beautiful, with tangled hair and a conical cap. Side view of the hat to the right. (Statuette figurine from Tylenos)

Conical hats on Egyptian bas-relief
http://www.ovnis.tv/noticias/2009/mayo/06mayII/cient_ruso.html
http://www.geocities.com/dominorus/atlantis.html

Pharaoh Akhenaton, from a statue in the library of the British Museum. The Pharaoh is equally a priest and a ruler, and wears the crown of the two halves (upper world and underworld) of his dominion. The lower crown denotes the upper world, the high conical hat the lower.

I tried to find a better explanation for all of these unusual things that happened to me in Egypt. Upon reading some information on the subject, I came to the conclusion that maybe the reflection of the two giants I saw in the Cheops Pyramid was due to my "psychometric ability".

According to Persi Fosset, "Any material object has a written memory of all its previous history". And people, who have this sensitive ability to feel this specific frequency, can read the message inscribed in these objects. The name given to the people who have this ability is "psychometrics". The famous blind psychic, Vanga, from Bulgaria was a real example of this. Before she met with scientists, she asked them to sleep the previous night with a crystal or a piece of sugar-crystal under their pillow, or with a watch with a Ruby crystal movement. The next morning she would take the crystal into her hand and read the person's information, which had been "transmitted" onto the crystal during the night. The famous Tofic Dadashev describes details of the life of the woman known as "The Jocund", through her portrait painted by Leonardo Da Vinci. The details of her life are only known by a small circle of specialists.

What about the room in the hotel when, as soon as I switched off the red lamp, these unusual voices of all these Egyptians animals and goddesses came out of the dark? On the one hand the memory of it is wonderful, yet, on the other hand, it really bothered me. I started studying the possible reason for which I heard these voices when I turned off the light.

I found that in 1851, Victor Hugo moved to a house he bought on the small island of Jersey in the North Sea. When he worked during the night he heard the sounds of a child running, a woman laughing, and that of a babysitter complaining. Every single night the same thing happened. No one ever saw any ghosts in that house. It seems that the walls of this house kept the sounds in their memory. The same happened to Persi Fosset in a "bad" house. As soon as he turned off the light, he heard screaming chicken running through his room and the sounds of an old, handicapped man following it. As soon as he turned the light on, the sounds disappeared. Every night this phenomenon repeated itself every time he switched the light off. He had strong nerves but he finally moved to a hotel when he could not stand it anymore. People who worked during the night in the Kremlin have heard sounds coming from the Lenin room during the last 80 years. This room is locked, but there are still sounds emanating from inside it, as if someone is moving furniture, or pacing the floor. It seems that these sounds have been created by ordinary activities, and not by a ghost. The same is true for The White House. Almost all American Presidents and members of their families have heard these kinds of sounds. Some even saw Abraham Lincoln, but in this instance, he did not produce any sound and did not move furniture.

According to numerous researches, in the dark, when people shut down their visual sensory perception, their hearing starts to be much more sensitive so that they effectively shut down the external background sounds from their hearing. They begin to accept what they hear and they start hearing faint, weak sounds. This can explain why people can hear things in the dark which they can't hear when a light is on in the room. When there is no light, we can start hearing sounds from the past which were preserved in the surrounding space, such as walls and various objects. Scientists think that in the future it may be possible for people not only to hear, but also to begin visualizing what they hear. This hypothesis was advanced by the science fiction author, Ivan Efremov. Well..., as for me it has already happened. I saw giants among normal size people near the pyramid!

According to Persi Fosset, who says that material objects have a written memory of all their previous history, rocks of the Cheops pyramid kept this motion picture with the two giants for thousands of years. And I can name myself as a psychometrics, because I feel this specific frequency!

When I delved into this subject a little deeper, I found that anyone could develop this ability. In Ukraine, Vecheslav Bronnikov developed a new method of "visual or hearing blindness". Normal kids began to read, have good orientation, recognized colors with closed eyes and their face covered with a black fabric.

Then I began to think that it may be possible to find some kind of mechanism to copy, from my eyes or my brain those visual scenes which I saw during hypnosis and in my visions. I really needed this sort of assistance when I started working with the artist who first drew the cover of this book.

I tried to explain to him a few times what I wanted but he just could not grasp (or visualize) what I was describing.

I saw a Priest, this 45- 50-year-old, wise, noble man with a kind heart, high cheekbones, tall, slim, but well built with a lean, beautiful muscle tone, with an enormous amount of jewelry around his neck and on his chest, hands and legs. I saw some tattoos on his face, a very unusual hair style with two pony tails and hundreds of small braids, with jewelry and feathers in it. He wore a jaguar coat. I saw his smiling, dark-blue eyes and his hand, tenderly caressing a white baby jaguar between its ears.

Instead, the artist drew a modern, urban man with drooping shoulders, with a fat belly. I tried to tell him that the Mayas had droughts at that time and they didn't have enough food to become obese. What's more, they were muscle-bound since they had to exercise a lot – even to accomplish a simple task. Imagine yourself walking up the pyramid a few times a day! You would be fit-and-trim in no time.

I also asked him to draw Kukulcan, the man-lizard, as in a Swarovski crystal toy-jewelry. Instead he drew a "vagrant" with green scales on his head and wrapped in a blanket.

Chak Mol is extremely tall, slim, a lean man playing with Maya boys.... Instead I got a modern, heavy punk-rock type of man, jumping on a stage....

Sadly, I understand that for modern people it is extremely difficult to imagine Atlantean body proportions, unless they see them in reality.

When I resumed my research a few weeks ago, I found an absolutely amazing invention, which would suit my needs perfectly! Since 1974, scientists have studied the hallucinations of mental patients and have endeavored to record what these patients saw – with astounding results. They placed a swimming mask in front of the patient's eyes, and a photo camera, focused on the eye of the patient, was fitted in place of the glasses. This camera was then able to photograph the eyes' reflection during their hallucination. The doctors, who performed this feat, began their study with 262 patients, from which they obtained 102 photos, displaying the visual hallucinations of their patients! The information was transferred from the brain to the optic nerve onto the eyes. Dr. Herbert, from England, called the nature of this type of stable light-flow a "bio-gravitation field" – not an electromagnetic field. I wish I had known about this technique before, so I could have shared with all of you exactly what I saw 2000 years ago in Chichen Itza.

Table of Common Characteristics

Common things in life; characters, habits, looks, interests, activities in the lives of the four people, who lived from 70 years, to 2 thousand and 10 thousand years apart from each other.

CHARACTERISTICS	AMELIA EARHART	JULIA SVADI HATRA	MAYA PRIEST	QUEEN OF ATLANTIS
Healing & Medicine	Yes	Yes	Yes	Yes
Basketball	Yes	Yes	Yes	No
Biology, agriculture, herbal plants	Yes	Yes	Yes	Possible
Math	Yes	Yes	Yes	Yes
Maps; land & sky	Yes	Yes	Yes	Possible
Airplanes, aviation, travel in space	Yes	Yes	Yes	Yes
Black hairy creatures *"Jabberwocky"*	Yes	Yes	Yes	
Love stars, addiction to the sky	Yes	Yes	Yes	Yes
Can't drink tea, coffee	Yes	Yes		
Tomato Juice	Yes	Yes		
Lougheed as an airplane & nurse's last name	Yes	Yes		
Hart and Hatra	Yes	Yes		
Flower named Amelia Jasmine Rose Lily	Yes	Yes		Possible
Twin trees with couples' names	Yes	Yes		
Leadership	Yes	Yes	Yes	Yes
High responsibility	Yes	Yes	Yes	Yes
Strength of character, brave nature	Yes	Yes	Yes	Yes
Responsible for the well-being of her people, society community	Yes	Yes	Yes	Yes
Hunting	Yes	Yes	Yes	
Ghost, Atchison "Most Ghostly Town in USA"	Yes	Yes	Yes	

CHARACTERISTICS	AMELIA EARHART	JULIA SVADI HATRA	MAYA PRIEST	QUEEN OF ATLANTIS
Curse	Yes	Yes	Yes	
Importance of numbers	Yes	Yes	Yes	Yes
Persistence and perseverance	Yes	Yes	Yes	Yes
Lots of followers, pioneers	Yes	Yes	Yes	Yes
Studying, sciences	Yes	Yes	Yes	Yes
Open new freedom and new possibilities	Yes	Yes		
Drowning	Yes	Yes	Unknown	Possible
Problems with own children	Yes	Yes	Yes	Yes
Worker in charge of children, teaching	Yes	Yes	Yes	
Big "ego"	Yes	No	Yes	No
Adoring Asia – Japan, China	Yes	Yes	Unknown	Yes
Fine Arts	Yes	Yes	Yes	Yes
Physics, studies the sounds of the rocks, energy, transportation	Yes	Yes	Yes	Yes
Music, sounds	Yes	Yes	Yes	Unknown
Poetry	Yes	Yes	Unknown	
Chemistry	Yes	Yes	Possible	
Zoology	Yes	Yes	Possible	
Pacifist	Yes	Yes	Unknown	Yes
Supreme intelligence	Yes	Yes	Yes	Yes
Same facial features	Yes	Yes	No	Yes
Deeply spiritual	Yes	Yes	Yes	Yes
Creativity	Yes	Yes	Yes	Yes
True love	Yes	Yes	Possible	Yes
Thick hair	Yes	Yes	Yes	Yes
Extensive travel	Yes	Yes	Possible	Possible
Martial Arts, tomboy	Yes	Yes	Yes	NO
Fear of "lost for ever"	Yes	Yes		
Younger sister	Yes	Yes		
Angry black dog	Yes	Yes		
Someone named Mary	Yes	Yes		
Girlfriends named Laura in school	Yes	Yes		
"Extreme" people in extreme situations	Yes	Yes	Yes	Yes

161

Amelia Reborn? Egypt

CHARACTERISTICS	AMELIA EARHART	JULIA SVADI HATRA	MAYA PRIEST	QUEEN OF ATLANTIS
Pilot shirt, similar clothing	Yes	Yes		
Astrology	Unknown	Yes	Yes	Yes
Jaguar skin, or print clothes		Yes	Yes	
Tortoise (turtle)		Yes	Yes	
White jaguar		Yes	Yes	
Connection with the Goddess, meeting with God		Yes	Yes	Yes
Word Caracol		Yes	Yes	
Word *Equinox* talking in ancient Maya		Yes	Yes	
Priesthood, priest's connection		Yes	Yes	Yes
Intuition, predictions	Yes	Yes	Yes	Yes
Masks		Yes	Yes	
Sacrifices		Yes	Yes	
Aztec God Xochipilli		Yes	Yes	
Addiction to crystals, growing crystals, diamonds, museums, factories		Yes	Yes	Yes
Playing the same "Rock from the past"		Yes	Yes	
Laser, X-ray technology, studied seeds		Yes	Yes	Yes
Book opening up like an accordion, website moving bar, business plan		Yes	Yes	
Spirit support		Yes	Yes	
Big, tall people		Yes	Yes	Yes
Materialization, teleportation, moving objects		Yes		Yes

I recognize now that I am lucky in life, because I had the rare possibility to see the chain of my past lives, the echoes from my past, and make adjustments to my future, spiritual development.

Conclusion

These four people had the same Spirit, which was transferred from the life of one person to the next and to the next. Skills, habits, experience, and knowledge accumulated in the Spirit holographic crystal are transferred with the Spirit to the next newborn person as an inheritance from all of his past lives. This is the chain of lives of people who carried the same Spirit. The Spirit of the people is ETERNAL.

****

Wow...! Suddenly, at the very moment I finished typing the last sentence of this book, this big, yellow and black butterfly flew from nowhere directly onto my laptop and sat right there, near the screen... I looked at the window... it was closed. It was cold outside. I was in shock and thinking, what is the time of the year now? It's still wintry – February!!! I don't know how it could be possible for this butterfly to appear so suddenly from nowhere in the middle of winter. Outside, there is still some snow in places in Stanley Park.

Amelia Reborn? Egypt

The last words that were on my mind, while I was creating this table, were *Materialization, teleportation, moving objects....* Was this the "Materialization" of a live butterfly? Or is this a gift to me from the ancient Spirits who supported me during the whole process of writing this book?

By coincidence, from today my whole book will be on the internet. It is now possible for everyone to read it...
Perhaps this wonderful butterfly was somewhere in my apartment, still in its cocoon, dormant from last summer? But what did it eat during its development into a caterpillar and into a full blown adult butterfly? No green leaves in the room – this is impossible! Surreal... Well, I believe it to be the work of the Spirit – same as *he* called three cars with the number 013 at the same time and at the same place and put them on the road one after the other. Same as it was *he* who sent my neighbor to bring his laptop out of the closet to put it near my door...

I clicked on the calendar of my laptop, it was February 19th, and took a photo of this gorgeous butterfly. I was still in shock, really, this kind of butterfly usually appears in Stanley Park at the end of June. I was still thinking about this outstanding situation, when I remembered a letter I received recently:

Hello Julia,

It's Mark Zealand, the documentary/camera man from English Bay.
I just wanted to say that I found our conversation very interesting, also very random!
One minute I'm filming people walking by, the next I'm listening to your unique story while an old man walks by with pigeons landing on his head!!

Well, I just wanted to say hello and if you want to talk some more about possible project ideas, let me know.
Cheers,
Mark

During the last three days, the butterfly sits on the corner of Tutankhamen's picture and I baby-sit her, feeding her honey water. They both have black and gold yellow stripes.

By the way, pharaohs have her blue eyelashes and even eyebrows... like Svadihatra from my dream and I myself have followed their fashion for the last 20 years.

Sources

1. The Miracle Man: The Life Story of João de Deus, by Robert Pellegrino-Estrich Extracted from his book Published in 1997, ©1997/1998 All Rights Reserve. Extracted from Nexus Magazine, Volume 5, #2 (February – March 1998). From our web page at: www.nexusmagazine.com

2. Paulo Coelho "Alchemistry" http://www.paulocoelho.com.br/russ/index.html

3. www.Atlantisoils.com, Atlantis oils, Healing & Well Being Centre

4. Zodiac Keywords, by Michael Erlewine http://lessons.astrology.com/course/show/Begin ners-Astrology/74-Zodiac-Keywords

5. Anubis statues, Copyright © 2006 The Unicorn Shoppe

6. Design by: IDEAS & Powered by Zen Cart theunicornshoppe.com/store/index.php?main_page/

7. Anubis http://www.google.ca/imgres?imgurl=http://dha whee.blogs.com/photos/uncategorized/anubis_st atue_1.jpg&imgrefurl=http://dhawhee.blogs.com/ d_hawhee/2007/01/index.html&h=360&w=288& sz=28&tbnid=4Ib2Z_lsGIYJ::&tbnh=121&tbnw=97 &prev=/images%3Fq%3DAnubis,%2Bstatue&hl=e n&sa=X&oi=image_result&resnum=3&ct=image&c d=1

8. Coneheads. Researcher Robert Connolly photographed this strange elongated skull in 1995. It was found in South America and is estimated to be tens of thousands of years old. http://www.light1998.com/Weird-Skeletons/Weird-Skeletons.htm

9. Joe Mills - http://www.light1998.com/ALIEN-SKULLS/ALIEN-SKULLS.htm

10. Dr. Gunther von Hagens, www.bodyworlds.com

10.   Buryl Payne, Discovery of biofield,
       http://newilluminati.blog-
       city.com/discovery_of_the_biofield.htm

11.   The Strange Disappearance of Amelia Earhart,
       Nostradamus and the New Prophecy Almanacs
       Michael McClellan.
       www.newprophecy.net/pastceleb.htm

Testimonials

Reading your book but I am crying so much reading I can hardly read it. Your book resonates so much with me, so much emotions it brings up. You put your heart in this book to touch the hearts of the readers.
Buryl Payne.

"I feel very close to Amelia when I look at you or read your words. She, as you know, was also a budding scientist-physician before she turned to flying planes. Amelia's survived spirit is a much more profound thing than any physical reality."
Todd.

Amelia here is just the top of the iceberg! Looks like the Spirit structure as a Russian doll "matreshka". Each layer is a human life and more deep it goes more ancient and unique person come out!!....Atlantean queen... Egyptian Royal Priest...Sumerian Priest.... and even Giants... But I agree, You, Svadihatra is the one who culminates with the final incarnation of this ancient Spirit Being as a scientist and author.
WISEWIND 1

Amelia Reborn displays living proof of how a profound spirit will live on through the ages, and re-manifest itself in other living beings. Maya Priest, Ancient Priest of Chichen Itza, Ancient Royal Egyptian, Sumerian Priest, Svadihatra, Giant Svadi, Atlantean woman, the chain is intertwined chronologically, to include Amelia and Julia, and no one tells it so beautifully as Amelia Reborn.
neilnils

I really do think from what I wrote that you are an amazing woman, someone that comes along once in a life time. You are a real live Goddess! Most priceless alive

human on the planet at our time. I really mean it is Incredible! Your outlook on life, philosophy and spiritual beliefs outstanding and intriguing. Your dreams very smart, unusual, bright and full of dynamic. It attracts like a magnet to read your wise book. Intelligence far beyond normal.
What is your IQ?
Henry D.

Amelia Reborn, her website, her spirituality, and her ever evolving outlook will truly and completely open the mind, the soul, and the spirituality of all who is not afraid to surrender themselves for their own self benefit.
ajajaj11113333

BEST BOOK TO TAKE TO THE BANKER! IT WILL BE NEVER BORING TO READ IT OVER AND OVER AGAIN FOR MANY YEARS! YOUR BOOK like a jewelry box for me, which if you would open it; you would be astonished seeing the flush of rare, magic multicolored things inside it. You are AVATAR who opened this rare knowledge to all of us.
hurrican888

I dreamed about you last night and the overall theme was: connected by the light and flying through space....
it made me very happy, I have had many past lives, also in Atlantis, Egypt etc., so no doubt we know each other.
Marianne Notschaele-den Boer
www.vorigelevens.nl

Wow! I guess I discovered real treasure here!
silvercrystall

This Spirit created the most longest commercial add in the history! With Amelia's disappearance mystery, Spirit keep whole world attention for 70 years long! And now decided

Amelia Reborn? Egypt

to give SECRET of SPIRIT's ETERNITY LIFE to humanity! Smart!
naturegene

That is so wonderful, and you should be so very proud of yourself. Just think of the impact that you can have on the lives of others through your book...opening up their minds, their spirituality, their soul, and their current lives!!!!!!"
Christopher M.

Afraid to die? Just read front page of that website! and you will never afraid again! Never! Can't wait to read whole book... Amazing! YES, Amelia alive! Can you believe it?
Miracleforest

Where to order the book or CDs:

For any information, please visit the website:
http://www.ameliareborn.com/
www.ameliareborn.com

Or contact me at:
contact@ameliareborn.com

YOU TUBE
amelia reborn
2012MayaPriest

To buy this or any of Julia SvadiHatra's five books on line, please visit Amazon.com, BarnesandNobles.com, Borders.com or ChapterIndigo.com and write the title of your choice in the "search window".

CD – available for purchase at
www.ameliareborn.com
　　1.　Reading – Amelia

Read More...

In the book, "**THE PRIEST**" you will find details of Julia's SPIRIT JOURNEY from her life as an Ancient Mayan Priest of Chichen Itza. 2000 years old secrets revealed: how he performed ceremonies and rituals on top of the pyramid, the Spirit world, sacrifices, symbols and the life of the ancient Maya people in Chichen Itza – a Message from them to the present-day civilization passed on to us. Meeting with God and angels, contacts with ancient Goddesses, Persian Goddesses, new Atharvan images, Zarathustra, ghosts, visiting a real Buddhist temple ... are all in Ancient Priest of Chichen Itza reincarnated by Julia SvadiHatra.

In the book, "**WHO IS CHAK MOL?**" you will find who the Ancient Priest meets in Chichen Itza! Guess who it was? A Mexican hero, Chak Mol! You will find out who he was; where he came from before arriving in Mexico and Chichen Itza and even who his mother was! He was a giant Atlantean man! You will find out where he lived and where he played in Chichen Itza.

In the book, "**KUKULCAN**" an Ancient Maya Priest comes to you through thousands of years and giving rare knowledge what you can expect after your own death. All people will live in Spirit world between lives. The spirit world is full of amazing colors, lights, dynamics speed and magic things which do not exist in our world. Travel in Time? Teleportation? Meeting with Kukulcan-Quetzalcoatl. Who is he? From where GIANTS come on Earth? Why people build pyramids? Do we live in the Past or in the Future?

In the book, "**THE REBIRTH OF AN ATLANTEAN QUEEN**" you will find the complete story about the Spirit Journey of Amelia and all her other past lives as a

Priest of Chichen Itza, an Atlantean Queen, Ancient Egyptian royal Priestess, Julia Svadihatra and even one future life. This big book contains all 4 books we just mentioned: Priest, Who is Chak Mol, Amelia Reborn, Kukulcan and an additional chapter: The Rebirth of an Atlantean Queen about life in Atlantis. Was Amelia an Atlantean Queen in her past life? Did she carry with her secrets of the crystal pyramid and how to re-ignite its energy? In this book Amelia's Spirit went back to her past life in Atlantis and her abilities began to emerge in this life time in a new re-born person!

Enjoy reading.

Exclusive editor of all 5 books:
Roxane Christ, www.1steditor.biz